British
English

Personal Best

A1 Beginner

Student's Book and **Workbook** combined edition

A

Series Editor
Jim Scrivener

Student's Book Author
Graham Fruen

Workbook Author
Daniel Barber

Richmond

STUDENT'S BOOK CONTENTS

Language App, unit-by-unit grammar and vocabulary games

Writing practice p64

My life

Hello

1 ▶ 1.1   Read and listen. Match conversations 1–3 with pictures a–c.

1 **Wendy** Good morning. Are you
Emma, the new teacher?
Emma Yes, I am.
Wendy I'm Wendy. Nice to meet you.
You're in Class 3.
Emma Thanks, Wendy. See you later.

2 **Emma** Hello, I'm Emma. What's
your name?
Kiko Hi, my name's Kiko.
Emma Nice to meet you, Kiko.
Kiko Are you a student here?
Emma No, I'm not. I'm your
teacher!

3 **Kiko** Emma, this is my friend,
Misha.
Emma Hello. Mmm, you aren't in
Class 3, Misha.
Misha No, I'm in Class 4 and I'm
late! Goodbye!
Emma Bye, Misha!

2 Put the words from the conversations in the correct columns. Can you add any other words?

Bye Good morning Hi See you later	Hello	Goodbye

3 A ▶ 1.2   Listen and repeat the highlighted phrases from the conversations in exercise 1.
How do you say them in your language?

B Practise the conversations from exercise 1 in groups of four.

4 A Complete the sentences with the words in the box. Then check your answers in the conversations.

're   'm   'm not   aren't   Are

1 I _____ Wendy.
2 You _____ in Class 3.
3 _____ you a student here?

4 No, I _____ .
5 You _____ in Class 3, Misha.

B ▶ 1.3   Listen and repeat the contractions in **bold**. Then read the Grammar box.

1 I am = **I'm**   2 You are = **You're**   3 You are not = **You aren't**

📖 **Grammar**   the verb *be* (*I, you*)

Positive:	Negative:	Questions and short answers:
I'm Wendy.	**You aren't** in Class 3.	**Are you** a teacher?
You're in Room 4.	**I'm not** a student.	Yes, **I am**. No, **I'm not**.

Go to Grammar practice: the verb *be* (*I, you*), page 96

5 A ▶1.5 Complete the conversation. Listen and check.

> **Kiko** Hello. What's ¹_____ name?
> **Eleni** ²_____ name's Eleni.
> **Kiko** Nice to ³_____ you, Eleni. I ⁴_____ Kiko.
> **Eleni** Nice to meet you, Kiko. ⁵_____ you a student here?
> **Kiko** ⁶ Yes, I _____ .

B In pairs, practise the conversation using your names.

6 Introduce yourself and your partner to another pair.

A *Hello, I'm Caro. This is Pablo.*
B *Nice to meet you. My name's Malika and this is Petra.*

7 ▶1.6 Read the phrases and write *Teacher* or *Student*. Listen and check.

1 _____
Open your books.

2 _____
Excuse me, what does 'late' mean?

3 _____
Sorry, I don't understand.

4 _____
Listen and repeat.

5 _____
How do you say 'buenos días' in English?

6 _____
Work in pairs.

Go to Vocabulary practice: classroom language, page 106

8 ▶1.8 **Pronunciation:** the alphabet Listen and repeat the sounds, words and letters.

/eɪ/	/iː/	/e/	/aɪ/	/əʊ/	/uː/	/ɑː/
late	meet	yes	my	no	you	class
Aa Hh Jj Kk	Bb Cc Dd Ee Gg Pp Tt Vv	Ff Ll Mm Nn Ss Xx Zz	Ii Yy	Oo	Qq Uu Ww	Rr

9 ▶1.9 Listen to the conversations. Write the names of the students.

Class 3
Student names:
1 _____
2 _____
3 _____

ABC
ABC School of English

Go to Communication practice: Student A page 134, Student B page 142

10 Introduce yourself to five students. Ask the questions and write the answers.

What's your name?   How do you spell that?

Personal Best Write a conversation between a teacher and a new student.

1A Where's she from?

1 A In pairs, match the flags with the countries.

A *What's a?*   **B** *I think it's Mexico.*

1 Argentina ____	3 China ____	5 Spain ____	7 the UK ____
2 Brazil ____	4 Mexico ____	6 Turkey ____	8 the USA ____

B ▶ 1.10 Listen, check and repeat.

2 A ▶ 1.11 Listen to the conversation. Repeat it in pairs.

> **A** Where are you from?   **A** Where's Salta?
> **B** I'm from Salta.   **B** It's in Argentina.

B In pairs, practise the conversation using the cities and countries.

> Toledo / Spain Izmir / Turkey Harbin / China York / the UK

> I'm from the UK.
> I'm British.

3 Look at the picture. Match the countries from exercise 1 with the nationalities.

1 British *the UK*	4 American _____	7 Turkish _____
2 Spanish _____	5 Argentinian _____	8 Brazilian _____
3 Mexican _____	6 Chinese _____	

Personal Best

Go to Vocabulary practice: countries and nationalities, page 107

4 ▶ 1.13 Do the quiz in pairs. Listen and check.

THE COUNTRIES QUIZ

1 What nationality is Lewis Hamilton?
a He's British.
b He's American.

5 Which sentence is correct?
a Sydney is the capital of Australia.
b Sydney isn't the capital of Australia.

2 Where is Mount Fuji?
a It's in China.
b It's in Japan.

6 Is *ceviche* Mexican or Peruvian?
a It's Mexican.
b It's Peruvian.

3 Is this elephant from India or Africa?
a It's from India.
b It's from Africa.

7 Where is the Bosphorus?
a It's in Turkey.
b It's in Russia.

4 Is Elsa Pataky Russian?
a Yes, she is.
b No, she isn't.

8 What nationality is Paulo Coelho?
a He's Italian.
b He's Brazilian.

5 A Match the pronouns *he*, *she* and *it* with the people and things.

1 he
2 she
3 it

a Elsa Pataky
b *ceviche*
c Lewis Hamilton

B Tick (✔) the form of the verb *be* that we use with *he*, *she* and *it*. Then read the Grammar box.

1 am ☐   2 is ☐   3 are ☐

📖 **Grammar** | **the verb *be* (*he, she, it*)**

Positive:
He's Japanese.
She's from Mexico.

Negative:
Barcelona isn't the capital of Spain.
She isn't Australian.

Questions and short answers:
Is it from India?
Yes, it is.   No, it isn't.

Personal Best

Go to Grammar practice: the verb *be* (*he, she, it*), page 96

6 A ▶ 1.15   **Pronunciation:** word stress Listen and repeat the words. Pay attention to the underlined stressed syllables.

Ja<u>pan</u>   Japa<u>nese</u>   <u>Mex</u>ico   <u>Mex</u>ican   <u>It</u>aly   <u>It</u>alian   <u>Tur</u>key   <u>Tur</u>kish

B ▶ 1.16   Underline the stress in the countries and nationalities. Then listen, check and repeat.

1 I'm Brazilian.   2 She's from Germany.   3 It's Chinese.   4 Is he from Argentina?

7 In pairs, ask and answer the question *Where's ... from?* about the people and things.

A *Where's Zara from?*   **B** *Is it Italian?*
A *No, it isn't. It's Spanish.*

Zara

Ryan Gosling

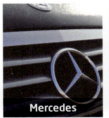
Mercedes

Thalía

Neymar

Chow mein

8 A ▶ 1.17   Listen and repeat the numbers.

0	1	2	3	4	5	6	7	8	9	10
zero/oh	one	two	three	four	five	six	seven	eight	nine	ten

B ▶ 1.18   What are the international dialling codes for the countries? Listen and write the answers.

1 China   + _____
2 Colombia + _____
3 India   + _____
4 Mexico   + _____
5 Spain   + _____
6 Turkey   + _____

Go to Communication practice: Student A page 134, Student B page 142

9 A In pairs, write six more quiz questions about countries and nationalities.

B Work with another pair. Ask and answer your quiz questions.

A *What is the capital of Wales? a) It's Glasgow. b) It's Cardiff.*
B *It isn't Glasgow – that's in Scotland. I think it's Cardiff.*
A *That's right! Your turn.*

Personal Best Write six sentences about people and things you like. Say where they are from.

1B Welcome to *Learning Curve*!

1 Match the jobs in the box with pictures a–f.

doctor   engineer   office worker   police officer   taxi driver   waiter

a   b   c   d   e   f

Go to Vocabulary practice: jobs, page 108

2 A ▶1.20   Look at the picture. Listen and complete the conversation.

A What's my job?
B Are you an ¹_____ ?
A No, I'm not. Try again!
B Are you a ²_____ ?
A Yes, I am.

B In pairs, play 'What's my job?'.

3 ▶1.21   Watch or listen to the start of a webshow called *Learning Curve*. Match the cities with the people.

1   New York   a   Simon, Kate, Marina
2   London   b   Ethan, Penny, Mohammed, Marc

🔧 **Skill**   listening for information about people

We often listen to information about people.
- Don't worry if you don't understand everything the speakers say.
- Read the questions and think about the information you need to listen for: name, job, nationality, etc.
- Listen for the verb *be*: *I'm … / He's … / She's …* etc.

4 ▶1.21   Read the Skill box. Watch or listen again and choose the correct information about the people.

Simon Collins
Nationality: British
Job: ¹ *TV presenter /
receptionist*

Ethan Moore
Nationality:
² *American / British*
Job: TV presenter

Penny Abernathy
Nationality:
English and
³ *Italian / Argentinian*
Job: TV presenter

Marina Ivanova
Nationality: Russian
Job: ⁴ *receptionist /
teacher*

Mohammed Bensallem
Nationality: American
Job: ⁵ *TV presenter /
office worker*

Marc Kim
Nationality: *American*
Job: ⁶ *doctor /
IT specialist*

Kate McRea
Nationality: ⁷ *American /
Argentinian*
Job: TV presenter

5 1.22 Watch or listen to the rest of the show. Who isn't in London now? Where is he/she?

Viktor

Sarah

Pedro

6 ▶1.22 Watch or listen again. Complete the information with countries and jobs.

1 Viktor: from: _____ job: _____ and _____
2 Sarah: from: _____ job: _____
3 Pedro: from: _____ job: _____

7 **A** In pairs, ask and answer the questions about the three people.

Where is … from? | What's his/her job?

B In pairs, ask and answer the questions about you.

Where are you from? | What's your job?

8 ▶1.23 Listen and read what Kate says. How does she say the contractions in **bold**? What do they mean?

> Hi, **I'm** Kate from *Learning Curve*. **What's** your name?

Listening builder | **contractions**

In English, we often use contractions, especially when we speak.
I'm from the United States. = ***I am*** from the United States.
*She **isn't** a student.* = *She **is not** a student.*
What's your job? = ***What is*** your job?

9 ▶1.24 Read the Listening builder. Listen and write the contractions.

1 _____ Spanish.   3 He _____ a doctor.   5 _____ an engineer.
2 _____ your name?   4 _____ from Japan.   6 The _____ here.

10 ▶1.25 In pairs, look at the pictures of Jia and Luis. Guess the information about the people. Listen to the conversations and check.

job? | nationality? | Where now?

Luis

Jia

11 Write the names of three friends or members of your family. In pairs, ask and answer questions about them.

A *Where's Saanvi from?*   **B** *She's from Nagpur.*
A *What's her job?*   **B** *She's an IT worker.*
A *Where is she now?*   **B** *She's in Mumbai.*

1C We are the champions

1 A Write the numbers in the box in the correct order.

> sixteen thirteen fourteen seventeen twelve twenty ~~eleven~~ fifteen nineteen eighteen

eleven, _____

B Look at the pictures and read the numbers. Tick (✔) the numbers that are correct.

1 twenty-three ☐   2 fifty-four ☐   3 eighty-six ☐   4 sixty-eight ☐   5 one hundred ☐   6 thirty ☐

Go to Vocabulary practice: numbers 0–100, page 111

2 A In pairs, ask and answer the question *How old is ...?* for the people in the picture.

A *How old is Kyle?*   B *I think he's 40.*

B ▶ 1.27 Listen and write the ages.

Kyle _____   Martin _____   Lorna _____

Kyle   Martin   Lorna

3 A Look at the picture. What do you know about the rock band Queen? Do you know any songs or the names of the band members?

B Read the introduction to the interview. What is the name of the band?

Queen for a night

No, this isn't a photo of Freddie Mercury and the rock band Queen. It's Dave Bryant, a teacher, and his band 'Queen for a night'. They're on a UK tour and tonight they're in Manchester. I'm with Dave and Jim from the band.

So Jim, are you all teachers?

Jim No, we aren't. I'm an engineer and Ed and Mick are doctors.

And where are you from?

Dave I'm from London, Jim and Ed are from Oxford and Mick's from Bristol. We're old friends from university.

How's the tour?

Jim It's good, but it's hard. It's a big tour – fourteen cities – and we aren't so young now!

Really? How old are you?

Dave Mick and I are forty-seven. And you and Ed are fifty …

Jim I'm not fifty! Ed's fifty … I'm forty-nine.

Dave Oh yes. Sorry, Jim!

And what's your favourite Queen song?

Dave That's easy! It's *We Are the Champions*!

4　▶1.28　Read and listen to the interview. Complete the information about the band.

	Dave	Jim	Ed	Mick
job				
city				
age				

5　**A**　Read the sentences from the interview. Match the people in **bold** with the pronouns *we*, *you* and *they*.

1 **Mick and I** are forty-seven. _____　　**2** **Jim and Ed** are from Oxford. _____　　**3** And **you and Ed** are fifty. _____

B　Tick (✔) the form of the verb *be* we use when we talk about more than one person.
Then read the Grammar box.

a *am / am not* ☐　　**b** *is / isn't* ☐　　**c** *are / aren't* ☐

> 📖 **Grammar**　**the verb *be* (*we, you, they*)**
>
> **Positive:**　　　　　　**Negative:**　　　　　　　　**Questions and short answers:**
> We**'re** old friends.　　We **aren't** young.　　　　　　**Are** you all teachers?
> They**'re** on a UK tour.　They **aren't** the rock band Queen.　Yes, we **are**.　No, we **aren't**.

Go to Grammar practice: the verb *be* (*we, you, they*), page 96

6　**A**　▶1.30　**Pronunciation:** numbers　Listen and repeat the numbers. Pay attention to how the stress changes.

1 a thir<u>teen</u>　**b** <u>thir</u>ty　　**2 a** four<u>teen</u>　**b** <u>for</u>ty　　**3 a** fif<u>teen</u>　**b** <u>fif</u>ty

B　▶1.31　Listen and tick (✔) the numbers you hear. Listen again and repeat.

1 a He isn't 16. ☐　**b** He isn't 60. ☐　　　**3 a** We aren't 17. ☐　**b** We aren't 70. ☐
2 a She's 18. ☐　　**b** She's 80. ☐　　　　　**4 a** They're 19. ☐　**b** They're 90. ☐

Go to Communication practice: Student A page 134, Student B page 142

7　Match adjectives 1–4 from the text with their opposites in the box.

> bad　small　old　difficult

1 young _____　　**2** good _____　　**3** big _____　　**4** easy _____

Go to Vocabulary practice: adjectives (1), page 109

8　Describe the pictures in pairs. Use positive and negative forms.

Picture a: They're big. They aren't small.

9　**A**　In small groups, imagine you are in a band and complete the table.

The name of the band	Your names	Your ages	Nationalities

B　Work with another group. Interview each other about your bands.

> What's the name of your band?　　What are your names?　　How old are you?　　Where are you from?

Personal Best　Write a short paragraph about a band you like.

1D What's your email address?

1 Match the places in the box with pictures a–c.

> hotel   car rental office   gym

2 **A** Look at the form. Match it with one of the pictures in exercise 1.

B ▶1.33 Listen to the conversation. Which piece of information in the form is **incorrect**?

Customer Information   *CARS-4-U*

Title	MR ☑ MRS ☐ MS ☐

Surname	Martin	First name(s)	Louis
Nationality	French	Date of birth	17/06/1980

Address	35 Rue Pasteur, Paris
Postcode	75099
email address	louis.martin@mymail.com
Phone number	33 1 80 26 58

🔧 **Skill** **completing a form**

When you complete a form, read all the instructions and sections carefully.
- Use the correct *title*. *Mr* = a man, *Mrs* = a married woman, *Ms* = a woman (married or unmarried).
- Your *surname* is your family name.
- Write your *date of birth* in numbers: the day/the month/the year: *13/09/1995*.
- For email addresses: @ = 'at' and .com = 'dot com'.

3 Read the Skill box. Match sections 1–9 with information a–i.

1	postcode	a	Smith
2	date of birth	b	M42 3GN
3	address	c	Ms
4	surname	d	s.smith@cjbrooks.com
5	first name	e	07700 900 357
6	email address	f	23/11/1988
7	title	g	British
8	phone number	h	Sarah
9	nationality	i	36 Charles Street, Manchester

4 In pairs, ask and answer questions about you, using the information in exercise 3.

A *What's your surname?*   **B** *It's Taylor.*
A *How do you spell that?*   **B** *It's T-A-Y-L-O-R.*

5 Look at answers a–i in exercise 3. Tick (✔) the information with capital letters.

1 first name ☐   3 email address ☐   5 street names ☐
2 surname ☐   4 nationality ☐   6 cities ☐

◀●▶ Text builder   capital letters

In English, we use capital letters (*A, B, C, D*, etc.) for the following:
- the first word in a sentence: *What's your name?*
- the personal pronoun *I*: *Hello, I'm Robert.*
- the names of people and places: *Emma is from Oxford.*
- countries, nationalities and languages: *We're from China. We're Chinese.*
- postcodes: *SN2 5EF*

---

6 A Read the Text builder. Find one **incorrect** capital letter in each sentence.

1 My friend Lena is American. She's From Florida.
2 Hello, I'm Antonio. I'm a new Student.
3 Our Address is 173 London Avenue, Manchester, M73 6XL.
4 This is Mesut. He's from Turkey and he's Twenty-one.

B Rewrite the sentences with capital letters.

1 what's his job? is he a doctor?   _____
2 my address is 3 white street, glasgow gl33 4sc.   _____
3 they aren't from germany. they're from poland.   _____
4 i'm your new english teacher. my name's jack.   _____

7 A PREPARE Look at the form. Check that you understand all the information you need to write.

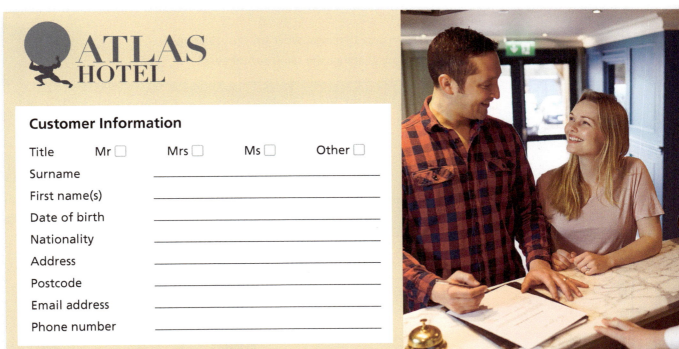

ATLAS HOTEL

Customer Information

Title   Mr ☐   Mrs ☐   Ms ☐   Other ☐
Surname   _____
First name(s)   _____
Date of birth   _____
Nationality   _____
Address   _____
Postcode   _____
Email address   _____
Phone number   _____

B PRACTISE Complete your form. Remember to use capital letters correctly.

C PERSONAL BEST Swap your form with a partner. Is it clear and easy to read? Are the capital letters correct?

Personal Best Design a form for a gym. Complete it with information about a family member.

People and things

2A The man with only 15 things

1 ▶ **2.1** In pairs, match the words in the box with objects a–f. Listen and check.

> a book   a bag   keys   a watch   an umbrella   a camera

 a
 b
 c
 d
 e
 f

Go to Vocabulary practice: personal objects, page 110

2 Look at exercise 1 and answer the questions. Then read the Grammar box.

1 Which noun do we use with *an*? _____   2 Which noun is plural? _____

📖 **Grammar**   **singular and plural nouns**

Singular nouns:	*a key*	*an umbrella*	*a watch*
Plural nouns:	*keys*	*umbrellas*	*watches*

Go to Grammar practice: singular and plural nouns, page 97

3 A Imagine you live with only 15 things. What are your 15 things?

B Read the text. Are your 15 things the same as Andrew's?

This Book is About **TRAVEL** A MODERN MANUAL 15 COUNTRIES WITH 15 THINGS ANDREW HYDE

15 countries *with* 15 things

This is Andrew Hyde, and that's his book: *15 countries with 15 things*. Andrew is from Colorado in the USA and he's a writer and traveller. And it's true – he's a man with only 15 things!

THESE ARE HIS 15 THINGS:

1 ___ bag	6 ___ wallet
2 ___ smartphone	7 ___ jacket
3 ___ camera	8 ___ trousers
4 ___ iPad	9 & 10 ___ shirts
5 ___ sunglasses	11 & 12 ___ shorts
13 ___ shoes	
14 ___ towel	
15 ___ wash bag	

Andrew is back in the USA now, but is he happy with just those 15 things? Yes, he says. Life is easy without a lot of things.

4 Look at the list of Andrew's things again. Write *a* or *an* for singular nouns, and – for plural nouns.

5 Complete the sentences from the text with the pronouns in the box. Which words do we use with singular nouns? Which ones with plural nouns? Then read the Grammar box.

> that   those   this   these

1 _____ is Andrew Hyde.
2 _____'s his book.
3 _____ are his 15 things.
4 Is he happy with just _____ 15 things?

> 📖 **Grammar**   *this, that, these, those*
>
> | Things that are near us: | Things that aren't near us: |
> |---|---|
> | **This** is my bag. | **That**'s my car. |
> | **These** are my keys. | **Those** are my friends. |

Go to Grammar practice: *this, that, these, those*, page 97

6 A ▶ 2.5 **Pronunciation:** /ɪ/ and /iː/ Listen and repeat the sounds and words.

| /ɪ/ | this | it | is | six |
| /iː/ | these | he | three | keys |

B ▶ 2.6 In pairs, say the sentences. Listen, check and repeat.

1 This is my city.
2 These are my keys.
3 Is that tree Japanese?
4 She's six and he's three.

Go to Communication practice: Students A and B page 135

7 Choose the correct words to complete the text.

What's in your bag?

Maria Clara, office worker, Rio de Janeiro

[1] *This / These* is my bag and [2] *this / these* are my things. This [3] *is / are* my book. It's in English! [4] *These / That* are my keys. [5] *This / These* key is for my house and [6] *that / those* key is for my car. [7] *This is / That's* my car over there – it's [8] *a / an* sports car! What's this? It's [9] *a / an* umbrella. It's very small! And the last thing? These are [10] *a / –* sunglasses!

8 A ▶ 2.7 Listen and match conversations 1–3 with pictures a–c.

a   b   c

B ▶ 2.7 Complete the phrases from the conversations with *this, that, these* and *those*. Listen again and check.

1 Jack   What's _____ ?
2 Woman   Jorge, who's _____ over there?
3 Man   Hi, Karen. What are _____ ?

Helen   _____ is my bag.
Jorge   _____'s Sergio.
Karen   _____ are my cameras.

9 Put some things from your bag on the desk. In pairs, ask and answer questions about the things.

A *What's that?*
B *This is a book. It's in Spanish.*
A *And what are those?*
B *These are my keys.*

Personal Best   Write about the things in your bag, as in exercise 7.

2B Lost!

1 A Match the words in the box with the colours.

> blue   brown   green   orange   pink   red

Go to Vocabulary practice: colours, page 110

B In pairs, point to objects in the classroom. Ask and answer *What colour is that/are those...?*

A *What colour are those books?*   **B** *They're orange.*

> **Skill** | **preparing to read**
>
> **Before you read a text, look at other information to help you prepare.**
> • Think about the style of the text. Is it from a magazine, a website, a letter?
> • Look at the pictures. What people, places and things can you see?
> • Read the title. What does it mean?

2 A Read the Skill box. What do you think the text on page 17 is about? Tick (✔) a, b or c.

a lost tourists in London ☐   **b** transport in London ☐   **c** lost objects in London ☐

B Read the text quickly and check your answer.

3 Read the text again. Are the sentences true (T) or false (F)?

1 The Lost Property Office is in London. ____
2 The objects are all from buses. ____
3 Tim Carlisle is a tour guide every day. ____
4 The laptop is new. ____
5 All the instruments are expensive. ____
6 The £15,000 is in the office now. ____

4 Complete the sentences with the words in the box. Check your answers in the text.

> expensive   violin   guitars   cheap

1 These _____ are _____ .   2 That's an _____ _____ .

> **Text builder** | **adjectives and nouns**
>
> adjective + noun: *£15,000 in a **brown envelope**.*
> noun + be + adjective: *This **laptop is new**.*
>
> **Look!** Adjectives don't change with plural nouns: *It's an **expensive instrument**. They're **expensive instruments**.*

5 Read the Text builder. Order the words to make sentences.

1 good it's a camera _____
2 sunglasses they're expensive _____
3 green bag the is _____
4 are the brown wallets _____
5 fast a it's car _____

6 A ▶2.9 Read and listen to the conversation in a Lost Property Office.

B In pairs, change the <mark>highlighted</mark> words and have a new conversation.

A Hello, can I help you?
B Do you have my wallet? It's a <mark>small, black wallet</mark>. It's <mark>expensive</mark>.
A One moment. Is this your <mark>wallet</mark>?
B Yes, that's it!

Lost in London

22,000 mobile phones, 12,000 credit cards, a green 'Incredible Hulk' toy, £15,000 in a brown envelope …

These are some of the things in the Transport for London Lost Property Office. Every year, 300,000 objects are lost on buses, trains and taxis in the city. I'm at the office in central London, and with me is Tim Carlisle. Tim is a worker here, but today he's my tour guide.

'Look at all these things – wallets, glasses, bags, shoes, mobile phones – they're all here,' Tim tells me. 'Look at this laptop – it's new.'

In a different part of the office are musical instruments. 'These guitars are cheap, but that's an expensive violin,' he says.

'What's over there?' I ask.

'Those are umbrellas. Big umbrellas, small umbrellas, blue umbrellas, pink umbrellas …'

'And what about the envelope with £15,000?' I ask. 'Is it still here?'

'No,' Tim says. 'An old man collected it last month. He's 80 years old and he doesn't like banks!'

And that's the end of my tour. It's time for me to go. Now, where's my phone?

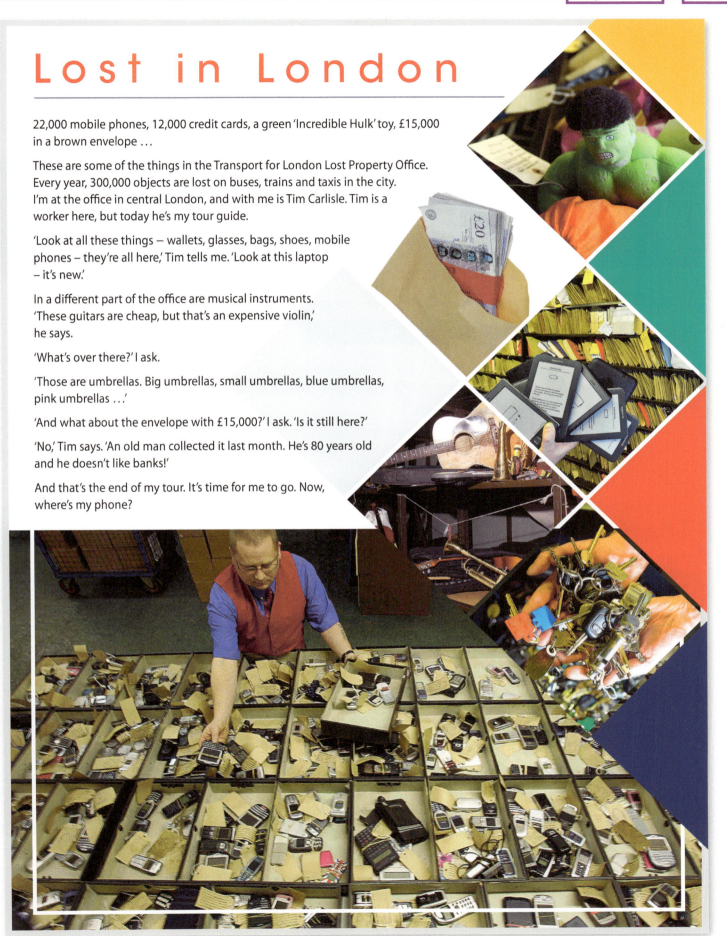

Personal Best   Write a conversation in a Lost Property Office.

2C My family

1 Match the people in the box with pictures a–d.

husband and wife   mother and son   father and daughter   brother and sister

2 Put the words from exercise 1 in the correct columns.

Male ♂	Female ♀
brother	*sister*

Go to Vocabulary practice: family and friends, page 111

3 A Discuss the questions in pairs.

1 Are you from a big family or a small family?
2 Do you live with your family?
3 Does anyone in your family live in a different city or country?

B Read the text quickly. What is Laura's family situation? Is she sad about it?

Long-distance families

Are you part of a 'long-distance' family? Are your brothers or sisters in a different city or country? Are you a long way from your parents or children? Tell us your stories.

Laura Wickham

Hi! My name's Laura. My husband Seamus and I are long-distance parents! We live in Cork in Ireland. Our daughter Amy is 30 years old and she's in Australia. Our son Conor is 26 years old and he's in the USA.
Amy and Conor are a long distance from us, but their lives are very interesting. Amy's an IT worker in Perth. Her husband Pete is from there. He's an engineer. Pete is Australian. Conor's a surfing teacher in Los Angeles. He loves California and its beautiful beaches, so it's his dream job! Conor's girlfriend Nicole is a Hollywood actor … well, that's her dream. At the moment, she's a waitress.
We're on Skype a lot with our children, but it's difficult with the time differences. Am I sad that they're so far away? Sometimes, but the important thing is that they're happy.

4 Read the text again. Match the information with the people.

1 This person is 30 years old.
2 This person is a waitress.
3 This person lives in Cork.
4 This person is a surfing teacher.
5 This person is Australian.

a Seamus
b Amy
c Pete
d Conor
e Nicole

5 Complete the sentences from the text with the words in the box.

> our   my   her   its   his   their

1 _____ name's Laura.
2 _____ son Conor is 26 years old.
3 _____ lives are very interesting.
4 _____ husband Pete is from there.
5 He loves California and _____ beautiful beaches.
6 It's _____ dream job!

6 A Choose the correct option to complete the sentence from the text.

Conor's / Pete's / Seamus's girlfriend Nicole is a Hollywood actor.

B What ending do we add to names and nouns to show possession? Read the Grammar box.

> **Grammar   possessive adjectives, 's for possession**
>
> **Possessive adjectives:**
>
> I — my: *I'm a teacher. **My** name's Karen.*
> you — your: *Are you OK? **Your** phone's broken.*
> he — his: *He's a tour guide. **His** job's interesting.*
> she — her: *She's Chinese, but **her** husband's British.*
> it — its: *Sydney's a great city. **Its** beaches are beautiful.*
> we — our: *We're in Class 3 and **our** teacher's very good!*
> they — their: *Jo and Ben aren't here. They're in **their** car.*
>
> **'s for possession:**
>
> **Kim's** mother is from Germany.
> Is this **Amy's** book?
> **My son's** new phone is expensive.

 Personal Best

Go to Grammar practice: possessive adjectives, 's for possession, page 97

7 A ▶ 2.12 **Pronunciation:** *'s* Listen and repeat. Pay attention to the 's sound.

son's   daughter's   Amy's   Conor's   my husband's   my sister's

B ▶ 2.13 In pairs, say the sentences. Then listen, check and repeat.

1 My husband's name is Felipe.
2 Our son's girlfriend is French.
3 My wife's parents are from Canada.
4 Sara's brother's girlfriend is a doctor.

Go to Communication practice: Student A page 135, Student B page 143

8 ▶ 2.14 Look at the people. In pairs, guess their relationship. Listen and check.

A *I think Jim is Tom Hanks's son.*   **B** *Yes, or maybe he's his brother.*

9 Choose five people in your family and write down their names. In pairs, ask and answer questions about the people.

A *Who is Azra?*   **B** *She's my brother's wife.*

> Who is he/she?   How old is he/she?   What is his/her job?

Personal Best Write a description of your family.

Learning Curve

2D What time is it?

1 A ▶ 2.15 In pairs, match the times in the box with the clocks. Listen and check.

five o'clock   ten past eight   quarter past ten   half past six   quarter to twelve   five to four

1 _____ 2 _____ 3 _____ 4 _____ 5 _____ 6 _____

B ▶ 2.16 Complete the times. Listen, check and repeat.

1 It's eleven _____ . 2 It's _____ three. 3 It's _____ twelve. 4 It's _____ nine.

2 A ▶ 2.17 Watch or listen to the start of *Learning Curve*. Choose the correct options to complete the sentences.

1 Kate is _____ .
   a at home **b** on holiday **c** at work
2 _____ are on the phone.
   a Kate's parents **b** Kate's friends **c** Kate's brothers
3 They are in _____ .
   a Boston **b** Los Angeles **c** London
4 Kate has _____ and a sister.
   a no brothers **b** one brother **c** two brothers

B ▶ 2.17 Watch or listen again and answer the questions.

1 What time is it in London? _____
2 What time is it in Los Angeles? _____

⬌ **Conversation builder** **telling the time**

Asking for the time:
What time is it? *What time's the film?*
What's the time? *What time's the next bus?*

Talking about times:
It's ten o'clock. *The film is at twenty past eight.*
It's seven a.m./p.m. *The bus is in ten minutes.*

---

3 A Read the Conversation builder. Match the questions with pictures a–d.

1 What's the time? _____
2 What time is *The Simpsons*? _____
3 What time is it in New York? _____
4 What time's the train to Birmingham? _____

B Ask and answer the questions in pairs.

4 ▶ **2.18** Watch or listen to the rest of the show. Match the times in the box with the people.

> 8.15   9.00   3.00   8.45   12.30

Man 1	Woman 1	Woman 2	Man 2	Simon
				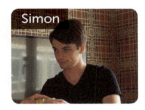

5 A ▶ **2.18** Match the questions with the people from exercise 4. Watch or listen again and check.

1 When's the match? _____
2 OK, what time is it? _____
3 Excuse me. What time's the James Bond film? _____
4 Excuse me. What time is it, please? _____
5 Where's the 67 bus? _____

B Which questions are polite? Why?

🔧 **Skill**   **asking for information politely**

When you ask for information, it's important to be polite.
• Use *Excuse me* or *Sorry* to get the person's attention.
• At the end of the conversation, say *Thank you* or *Thanks*.
• If you want to be extra polite, say *Please* at the end of questions.

---

6 ▶ **2.19** Read the Skill box. In pairs, guess the missing words from the conversations. Listen and check.

Woman 1 ¹_____ . What time is it, ²_____ ?
Kate It's 8.15. Quarter past.
Woman 1 Oh! I'm late. ³_____ very much.

Woman 2 ⁴_____ , what time is the 67 bus?
Kate Next bus ... 8.45. It's in ten minutes.
Woman 2 Oh, 8.45, not 8.35. Ten minutes. OK. ⁵_____ .

7 In pairs, practise asking for information politely.

Questions	Answers
what / the teacher's name	It's Leanne.
what time / next bus to Cambridge	It's at 12.20 p.m.
where / the museum	It's that building.
what / name of this restaurant	It's The Golden Dragon.
what / the school's phone number	It's 354 269.

Go to Communication practice: Student A page 135, Student B page 143

8 A PREPARE In pairs, choose the cinema or the airport and invent the missing information.

★ SILVER CINEMA ★

FILM	TIME	SCREEN
Star Wars	_____	_____
Titanic	_____	_____
The Wizard of Oz	_____	_____

Airport departures ✈   `10:05`

Flight	Time	Gate
Stockholm	_____	_____
Beijing	_____	_____
Lima	_____	_____

B PRACTISE In pairs, ask and answer questions about the films or the flights. Remember to be polite.

C PERSONAL BEST Invent information for the other situation and repeat the activity. Is your speaking better this time?

Personal Best Write a conversation with a tourist in your local train or bus station.

Grammar

1 Choose the correct options to complete the sentences.

1 Hi Laura, I _____ Khalid's brother. Nice to meet you.
   a 's
   b 're
   c 'm

2 How old _____ your grandfather?
   a are
   b is
   c am

3 _____ these your glasses?
   a Am
   b Is
   c Are

4 A Is your sister's boyfriend from Brazil?
   B No, _____ .
   a he isn't
   b she isn't
   c I'm not

5 A What's this?
   B It's _____ old book.
   a –
   b a
   c an

6 _____ my mother over there with the blue umbrella.
   a These are
   b This is
   c That's

7 My wife's a chef and this is _____ new restaurant.
   a she's
   b her
   c his

8 My _____ surname is Chen.
   a grandfather's
   b grandfather
   c grandfathers

2 Rewrite the sentences with the new words.

1 He's an English teacher.
   They *'re English teachers* .

2 These are my red pens.
   This _____ .

3 We're happy with our new tablets.
   I _____ .

4 Those expensive cars are Italian.
   That _____ .

5 I'm a student in India.
   She _____ .

6 My brother's an office worker and this is his bag.
   My brothers _____ and
   these _____ .

3 Choose the correct options to complete the text.

A HOLLYWOOD FAMILY

[1] *These / This* is Zooey Deschanel. She's [2] *a / an* actor and a singer. [3] *She / Her* sister Emily is an actor too. She's in the TV show *Bones*. What [4] *'s / 're* their mother's job? An actor. And [5] *their / our* father's job? [6] *Her / His* job is in films too! That's not all – Zooey's [7] *sister's / sisters* husband is … an actor.
They [8] *'re / 's* from California in the USA and they're a Hollywood family. They [9] *are / aren't* the only family like this. From Marlon Brando's family to Will Smith's family, they [10] *'m / 're* easy to find in Hollywood.

Vocabulary

1 Put the words in the box in the correct columns.

> ~~difficult~~ engineer grandfather interesting
> IT worker mobile phone mother pencil
> receptionist small watch wife

Jobs	Adjectives	Family	Personal objects
	difficult		

2 Circle the word that is different. Explain your answers.

1 black   new   orange   gold
2 chef   tour guide TV presenter grandmother
3 French   Polish   Russian   Canada
4 fifty   thirteen   fourteen   seventeen
5 son   glasses   purse   keys
6 Hi   Bye   Hello   Good morning
7 bad   boring   ugly   happy
8 father   daughter   boyfriend   husband

3 Choose the correct options to complete the sentences.

1 Jing Wei is _____ . She's from Shanghai.
   a doctor   b Chinese   c brother
2 Excuse me, what does 'building' _____ ?
   a say   b understand   c mean
3 My sister's daughter is six and her _____ is four.
   a son   b children   c husband
4 That camera is very _____ .
   a new   b young   c sad
5 Russia is a very _____ country.
   a small   b easy   c big
6 I'm from _____ . I'm American.
   a the UK   b the USA   c Argentina
7 **A** It's ten past nine.
   B Sorry I'm _____ .
   a student   b teacher   c late
8 Macu is a _____ . She's in her car all day.
   a shop assistant b taxi driver c girlfriend
9 **A** What colour is a chef's hat?
   B It's _____ .
   a white   b small   c pink
10 The pages of this old _____ are yellow.
   a tablet   b wallet   c book

4 Complete the conversation with the words in the box.

> nineteen   Germany   Italian   waitress
> bag   student   girlfriend   later

Max Who's that girl with Frank? Is she his sister?
Sue No. That's his new ¹_____ .
Max Wow! Is she from here?
Sue No, she's from ²_____ .
Max She's beautiful. How old is she?
Sue She's ³_____ .
Max Is she a ⁴_____ at the university?
Sue No, she's a ⁵_____ at the ⁶_____
          restaurant in Green Road.
Max Oh no, I'm late for class. See you ⁷_____ .
Sue Hey ... is that your ⁸_____ ?
Max Yes, it is. Thanks!
Sue Bye.

Personal Best

Lesson Hello
Write a phrase to introduce a friend to someone.

Lesson 2A
Name four objects in your bag.

Lesson 1A
Name five nationalities, but not your own.

Lesson 2A
Describe one of your personal objects.

Lesson 1B
Describe someone, including their job and nationality.

Lesson 2B
Write two of your favourite colours.

Lesson 1B
Write three questions to ask a new student in your class.

Lesson 2B
Describe something in the classroom.

Lesson 1C
Write the ages of three people in your family.

Lesson 2C
Write two sentences about people in your family.

Lesson 1D
Write three words that always start with capital letters.

Lesson 2D
Write what time it is now.

Food and drink

LANGUAGE   present simple (*I, you, we, they*) ■ food and drink

3A Food for athletes

1 ▶ **3.1**   Put the words in the box in the correct columns. Listen and check.

eggs   orange juice   meat   tea   coffee   bread   rice   water

We eat …	We drink …

Personal Best

Go to Vocabulary practice: food and drink, page 112

2 In pairs, talk about food and drink that you like and don't like.

🙂 *I like meat.*   ☹ *I don't like coffee.*

3 A Look at the pictures. What food can you see? Is it healthy?

B Match pictures a and b with the athletes. Read the text quickly and check.

Olympic Diets   What do Olympic athletes eat for breakfast, lunch and dinner? We talk to two very different athletes.

a

b

Artem Petrenko, Weightlifter, Ukraine

What do you eat for breakfast?
For breakfast, I eat six eggs and three or four cheese sandwiches. I drink a litre of orange juice and three cups of coffee.

What about lunch and dinner?
I have lunch at 1.00 p.m. I eat a big bowl of pasta or rice and salad. For dinner, I eat meat – with potatoes and vegetables. During the day, I eat more sandwiches and fruit.

That's a lot of food! What's your favourite food?
Cheese. I love all cheese, and my favourite is Dutch cheese, like Gouda.

Michelle Nelson, Marathon runner, Australia

What do you eat for breakfast?
For breakfast, I eat brown bread and fruit and I drink 'green juice' – it's juice with green vegetables and fruit. I'm a vegan, so I don't eat meat, eggs or fish and I don't drink milk.

What about lunch and dinner?
For lunch, I have a vegan burger with rice and salad. In the evening, I have dinner with my family. It's difficult because we don't like the same things! But we all eat pizza. My two sisters like cheese, but I have a vegan pizza – without cheese!

Do marathon runners eat dessert?
Yes, they do! Well, maybe not all of them … but I love dessert. It's my favourite part of the meal. I love carrot cake and vegan ice cream.

4 Read the text again and complete the sentences with the correct words.

1 What _____ you _____ for breakfast?
2 I _____ a litre of orange juice.
3 I _____ lunch at 1.00 p.m.
4 I _____ milk.
5 We _____ the same things.
6 _____ marathon runners _____ dessert?

5 A Look at the sentences in exercise 4 and answer the questions.

1 Which sentences are positive? _____ and _____
2 Which are negative? _____ and _____
3 Which are questions? _____ and _____

B Complete the rules. Then read the Grammar box.

1 We use _____ + verb in negative present simple sentences with *I, you, we* and *they*.
2 We use _____ + subject + verb in present simple questions with *I, you, we* and *they*.

📖 **Grammar**   **present simple (*I, you, we, they*)**

Positive:	Negative:	Questions and short answers:
I **drink** a lot of water.	You **don't drink** coffee.	**Do** you **like** fish?
We **eat** ice cream for dessert.	They **don't like** vegetables.	Yes, I **do**. No, I **don't**.

Go to Grammar practice: present simple (*I, you, we, they*), page 98

Personal Best

6 ▶ 3.4 **Pronunciation:** *do you* /djuː/ Listen and repeat the questions. Pay attention to the pronunciation of *do you* /djuː/.

1 Do you like pizza?   2 What do you eat for breakfast?   3 What food do you like?

7 A ▶ 3.5 Say the questions. Listen, check and repeat.

1 Do you like Mexican food?
2 Do you eat meat?
3 Do you drink tea?
4 Do you like chocolate?
5 What time do you have breakfast?
6 What do you have for lunch?

B Ask and answer the questions in pairs.

8 A ▶ 3.6 Complete the text with the verbs in brackets. Listen and check.

Happy food

What food [1]_____ (you / like) after a difficult day? What [2]_____ (you / eat) when you're sad? What's your 'happy food'?

I'm a student. After a difficult day at university, [3]_____ (we / always have) ice cream. [4]_____ (I / like) caramel – it's my favourite!

Harriet, the UK

My children are strange. [5]_____ (they / not like) normal sandwiches. [6]_____ (they / eat) banana and cheese sandwiches!

Mike, Canada

I'm a doctor. When I'm tired or sad, [7]_____ (I / not eat) chocolate or pizza – it's bad for you. [8]_____ (I / drink) green tea.

Rosa, Argentina

B In pairs, talk about your 'happy food'. What do you eat or drink when you're sad or tired?

Go to Communication practice: Student A page 136, Student B page 144

9 A Ask and answer questions in pairs.

1 like / Japanese food
2 drink / a lot of soft drinks
3 have / dinner with your family
4 eat / a lot of fruit
5 drink / coffee at night
6 eat / a lot of red meat

A *Do you like Japanese food?*   **B** *No, I don't. But I like Indian food.*

B Tell the class what you and your partner have in common.

We don't like Japanese food, but we like Indian food.

Personal Best   Write what you have for breakfast, lunch and dinner on a typical day.

Learning Curve

3B Tea or coffee?

1 Complete the café sign with the days of the week.

Friday   Tuesday   Wednesday   Sunday

Riverside Café

We are open:

Monday	Closed	
1 _____	9.00 a.m.–5.00 p.m.	
2 _____	9.00 a.m.–5.00 p.m.	
Thursday	Closed	
3 _____	9.00 a.m.–9.00 p.m.	
Saturday	10.00 a.m.–11.00 p.m.	
4 _____	10.00 a.m.–4.00 p.m.	

Hot food & sandwiches!
Coffee & cake!

Personal Best

Go to Vocabulary practice: days and times of day, page 116

2 Look at the sign in exercise 1 again. Are the sentences true (T) or false (F)?

1 The café is open every day. _____
2 It's open in the morning on Tuesday. _____
3 It's open on Thursday afternoon. _____
4 It's open in the evening on Friday. _____
5 It's closed on Saturday night. _____
6 It's closed in the evening on Sunday. _____

3 Ask and answer the questions in pairs.

1 What day is it today?
2 What day is it tomorrow?
3 What day was it yesterday?
4 What's your favourite day of the week?
5 What's the worst day of the week?
6 What's your favourite time of day?

4 A ▶ 3.8 Watch or listen to the first part of the show. Tick (✔) the sentence which is correct.

1 People drink coffee in cafés and tea at home. ☐
2 People drink tea and coffee all over the world. ☐
3 People drink coffee in the morning and tea in the evening. ☐

Learning Curve

B ▶ 3.8 Watch or listen again. Match the halves to make sentences.

1 54% of Americans
2 65% of those people
3 35% of those people
4 In the UK, people drink 165 million
5 In the UK, people drink 70 million

a cups of tea every day.
b drink coffee at lunch or later.
c drink coffee every day.
d drink coffee in the morning.
e cups of coffee every day.

5 ▶ 3.9 Watch or listen to the second part of the show. Match the people with the food and drink.

Jolene

Ioan

Chan

Ethan

Kate

1 fish, rice, vegetables, tea, water _____
2 biscuits, ice cream, coffee _____
3 fish and chips and tea _____

4 sandwich, crisps, biscuit, tea _____
5 coffee, cereal _____

⚒ Skill   listening for times and days

Listen carefully when people talk about times and days.
- Times and days can come at the beginning or end of a sentence: *On Friday, I go to the café. / I go to the café on Friday.*
- Some times and days sound similar: *It's three fifteen. / It's three fifty.   Today is Tuesday. / Today is Thursday.*

---

6 ▶ 3.9 Read the Skill box. Watch or listen again and choose the correct options to complete the sentences.

1 **Kate:** It's *2.30 p.m. / 2.40 p.m.* here and I'm with Jolene.
2 **Jolene:** We come here every *Tuesday / Thursday*. It's my husband's favourite café.
3 **Jolene:** I drink coffee every *morning / evening*, but between 2.30 and *3.00 / 3.30*, I drink tea.
4 **Ioan:** The party's at *8.00 p.m. / 9.00 p.m.*
5 **Chan:** We're open *Monday / Sunday* through Friday from 11.00 a.m. until 10.00 p.m. And Saturday and Sunday from 10.00 a.m. until *7.00 p.m. / 11.00 p.m.*
6 **Kate:** It's *3.15 / 3.30* here and I have fish and chips from my favourite takeaway place!

---

7 In pairs, talk about what food and drink you have every day.

I have a coffee at 10.00 in the morning.

8 ▶ 3.10 Listen to the extract from the show. How does Ethan pronounce *and*?

> I have a coffee **and** cereal.

🧩 Listening builder   the sound /ə/

The /ə/ sound is also called 'schwa'. It is very common in English in short unstressed words, like articles, prepositions and auxiliary verbs.

/ə/ /ə/   /ə/   /ə/   /ə/
a cup of tea   *We have coffee at 9.00 p.m.*   *What time's the party?*   *Does she like fish?*

---

9 ▶ 3.11 Read the Listening builder. Then listen and complete the sentences.

1 I have _____ coffee every morning.
2 What _____ they eat?
3 They only drink tea _____ breakfast.

4 This one's _____ you.
5 I have two bottles _____ water.
6 I like fish _____ chips.

10 Think of a café that you like. In pairs, ask and answer the questions about the café.

What's its name?   Where is it?   When do you go there?

What do you eat or drink there?   What do other people have?   Why do you like it?

3C Chocolate for breakfast!

1 Complete phrases 1–6 with the verbs in the box.

use   watch   have   do   make   say

1 _____ 'hello'   **2** _____ a cat   **3** _____ dinner   **4** _____ exercise   **5** _____ a computer   **6** _____ TV

Personal Best

Go to Vocabulary practice: common verbs (1), page 113

2 Ask and answer the questions in pairs.

1 you / live near the city centre?
2 you / work in an office?
3 you / make dinner at home every evening?
4 you / know three languages?
5 you / say 'hello' to a lot of people every day?
6 you / have brothers or sisters?

3 ▶ 3.13 Look at the picture of Adam Young. What is his job? Read and listen to the text and check.

THE BEST JOB IN THE WORLD?

From Monday to Friday, Adam Young eats chocolate at work. That's because Adam is a *chocolatier* (he makes chocolate). 'I love it,' he says. 'I think it's a great job!'
Adam lives in Perth in Scotland. He has a small shop and he makes all of his chocolates by hand. Does he have the best job in the world? This is his typical day.
'In the morning, I go to the shop early and make chocolate … I eat it for breakfast! Then we work here all day.'

Adam has an assistant, Shona. When he's in the kitchen with the chocolate, Shona works with the customers.
Adam does a lot of exercise – very important when you eat chocolate all day!
In the evening, he changes his clothes and goes to the gym. Then he goes home, makes dinner and watches TV.
At the weekend, he studies Business – he says it's important for his job … but he doesn't eat chocolate!

4 A Choose the correct words to complete the sentences. What letter do we add to the verbs with *he*, *she* and *it* in positive sentences?

1 Adam Young *eat / eats* chocolate at work.
2 He *make / makes* all of his chocolates by hand.
3 I go to the shop early and *make / makes* chocolate.
4 I *eat / eats* it for breakfast!
5 Then we *work / works* here all day.
6 Shona *work / works* with the customers.

B Find the *he*/*she*/*it* forms of the verbs in the text.

1 say _____
2 live _____
3 have _____
4 do _____
5 change _____
6 go _____
7 watch _____
8 study _____

5 Find a question and a negative sentence in the text. Complete the rules then read the Grammar box.

1 We use _____ + verb in negative present simple sentences with *he/she/it*.

2 We use _____ + subject + verb in present simple questions with *he/she/it*.

📖 **Grammar**   **present simple (*he, she, it*)**

Positive:
*She **eats** fruit for breakfast.*
*He **watches** TV in the evening.*
*Maya **studies** English.*

Negative:
*He **doesn't work** in a school.*
*She **doesn't do** exercise.*
*My wife **doesn't like** chocolate.*

Questions and short answers:
***Does** your house **have** a garden?*
*Yes, it **does**.   No, it **doesn't**.*

Look! Some verbs are irregular: *do > **does**, go > **goes**, have > **has**.*

Go to Grammar practice: present simple (*he, she, it*), page 98

6 A ▶ 3.15 **Pronunciation:** -*s* and -*es* endings Listen and repeat the sounds and words. Pay attention to the pronunciation of the -*s* and -*es* endings.

1	/s/	eats	works	makes
2	/z/	lives	goes	knows
3	/ɪz/	watches	uses	changes

B ▶ 3.16 Match the halves to make sentences. Listen, check and repeat.

1 She lives   a films in the afternoon.
2 He works   b in an office.
3 She watches   c a computer at work.
4 He says   d 'Hi' every day.
5 She makes   e in Tokyo.
6 He uses   f cakes at the weekend.

7 ▶ 3.17 Complete the text with the correct form of the verbs in the box. Listen and check.

have do eat say work make go

A VERY COOL JOB

Kirsten Lind ¹_____ at an ice cream company in Toronto. She ²_____ a great job – she's a food scientist and she ³_____ new flavours of ice cream. What's this week's new flavour? 'Potato crisps and chocolate! I don't like crisps, but lots of people love it,' Kirsten ⁴_____ . Kirsten ⁵_____ two or three litres of ice cream a week, so she ⁶_____ to the gym after work and she ⁷_____ a lot of sport at the weekend.

8 A Make questions about the text in exercise 7.

1 Kirsten / work / in a shop?   _____
2 she / have / an interesting job?   _____
3 she / eat / a lot of crisps?   _____
4 she / do / a lot of exercise?   _____

B Ask and answer the questions in pairs. Use short answers.

Go to Communication practice: Student A page 136, Student B page 144

9 Choose three friends or family members and write down their names. Ask and answer the questions in pairs.

A *Who is Ivan?*   **B** *He's my uncle.*
A *Where does he live?*   **B** *He lives in ...*

Who is ... ?   Where does he/she live?   Where does he/she work?

Does he/she like his/her job?   What does he/she do at the weekend?

Personal Best   Think of someone with an interesting job and write a paragraph about him/her.

3D A special meal

1 **A** Match the food in the box with the festivals in the pictures. What do you know about these festivals?

pancakes   chow mein   turkey   sweets

Thanksgiving, USA

Carnevale, Italy

Chinese New Year, China

Maslenitsa, Russia

B Think of some important festivals and celebrations in your country. What do people eat and drink?

2 Look at the pictures in Arusha's blog. Which country is she from? How do people celebrate this festival? Read the text quickly and check.

Arusha's Blog

MY POSTS | CONTACT ME | SEARCH

About me
Hi! I'm Arusha, I'm 25 and I live in Kerala in India. Welcome to my blog!

Festival time

We have lots of festivals in India and my favourite is Onam.

In the afternoon, we have a big meal with lots of food – some people have 24 dishes or more. We eat curry, rice, vegetables and fruit, but we don't eat meat. We eat the food on a big banana leaf.

It's traditional to have lunch at home, but these days some people go to restaurants. In my family, we eat at my brother's house. After the meal, we meet friends, we listen to music and we watch the tiger dance. What's my favourite thing about Onam? It's a really happy time and the food is great.

3 Read the text again and answer the questions.

1 What is the name of the festival?
2 When do people have the meal?
3 What food does Arusha eat?
4 What doesn't she eat?
5 Where does she have lunch?
6 What does she do after the meal?

4 Read the Skill box. Find an example of each type of punctuation in the text on page 30.

🔧 Skill   punctuation

It's important to use the correct punctuation to help people understand your writing.

.	**full stop:**	We use this at the end of a sentence.
,	**comma:**	We use this to separate ideas and after times.
?	**question mark:**	We use this at the end of a question.
'	**apostrophe:**	We use this in contractions and in *'s* for possession.
A	**capital letters:**	(see the Text builder on page 13)

5 Rewrite the text about Chinese New Year with the correct punctuation and capital letters.

whats your
favourite festival

my names wu and im from nanjing in china my favourite festival is chinese new year its a national holiday and people dont work we have a big party with all the family and in the evening we eat meat fish rice and vegetables my mother makes a special cake and we give money to the children in the family

6 Choose the correct words to complete the sentences from Arusha's blog. Check your answers in the text.

1 We eat curry, rice, vegetables and fruit, *and / but* we don't eat meat.
2 It's a really happy time *and / but* the food is great.

⟮⟯ Text builder   linkers (*and, but*)

We use *and* and *but* to link sentences.
To add information: *We dance **and** we listen to music.*
To contrast different ideas: *Some people go to restaurants, **but** our family eats at home.*

7 Read the Text builder. Complete the sentences with *and* or *but*.

1 We go to my grandmother's house every Sunday _____ we have a big meal.
2 This restaurant is very expensive, _____ the food isn't good.
3 I drink tea and fruit juice, _____ I don't drink coffee.
4 Claire works in the morning, _____ she doesn't work in the afternoon.
5 My uncle lives in Los Angeles, _____ he isn't American.
6 He does sport _____ he goes to the gym.

8 A **PREPARE** Choose a festival in your country where food is important. Think about these questions.

• When is the festival?
• What do people eat and drink?
• Where do you eat and who with?
• What do you do before and after the meal?

B **PRACTISE** Write a blog about the festival. Link your sentences with *and* and *but*.

C **PERSONAL BEST** Swap your blog with your partner. Check the grammar and punctuation.
Are the present simple verbs correct? Does your partner use *and* and *but* correctly?

Personal Best Think of a special meal. Write three sentences about it with *and* and three sentences with *but*.

Daily life

4A Day and night

1 A ▶ 4.1   Match the phrases in the box with pictures a–e. Listen and check.

start work   finish work   go to bed   get home   get up

B In pairs, say what time you do the activities.

A *I get up at 6.30.*   **B** *That's early! I get up at 8.30.*

Go to Vocabulary practice: daily routine verbs, page 114

2 Look at the pictures and guess the answers to the questions. Read the text and check.

1 What is the relationship between the two people?
2 What are their jobs?
3 Are their routines similar or different?

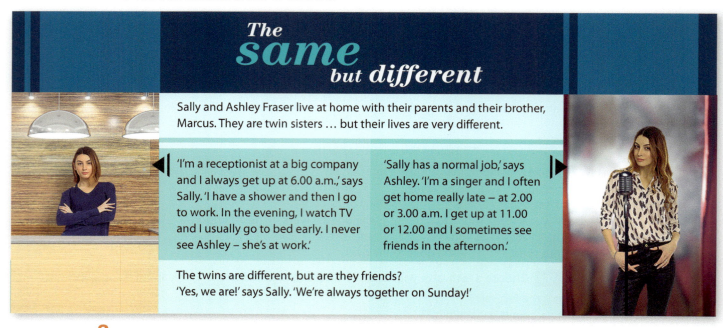

The same but different

Sally and Ashley Fraser live at home with their parents and their brother, Marcus. They are twin sisters … but their lives are very different.

'I'm a receptionist at a big company and I always get up at 6.00 a.m.,' says Sally. 'I have a shower and then I go to work. In the evening, I watch TV and I usually go to bed early. I never see Ashley – she's at work.'

'Sally has a normal job,' says Ashley. 'I'm a singer and I often get home really late – at 2.00 or 3.00 a.m. I get up at 11.00 or 12.00 and I sometimes see friends in the afternoon.'

The twins are different, but are they friends?
'Yes, we are!' says Sally. 'We're always together on Sunday!'

3 Complete the sentences with the adverbs of frequency in the box. Check your answers in the text.

always   sometimes   usually   never   often

1 I _____ see Ashley.
2 I _____ see friends in the afternoon.
3 I _____ get home really late.
4 I _____ go to bed early.
5 I _____ get up at 6.00 a.m.

4 **A** Put the adverbs of frequency in the box in the correct order.

> sometimes   usually   never

100% ▬▬▬▬▬▬▬▬▬▬▬▬▬▬▬▬▬▬▬▬▬▬▬▬▬▬▬▬▬▬▬ 0%

always   1 _____   often   2 _____   3 _____

B Read the sentences in exercise 3 again. Do the adverbs of frequency come before or after the verbs? Read the Grammar box.

📖 **Grammar**   **adverbs of frequency**

100% 🔻
always:	I **always** have breakfast at home.
usually:	She **usually** has a shower in the morning.
often:	I **often** get up late at the weekend.
sometimes:	I **sometimes** get home at 1.00 a.m.
0% | **never:** | She **never** has dinner at home. |

Look! Adverbs of frequency come after the verb *be*: *We're **always** together on Sunday.*

Go to Grammar practice: adverbs of frequency, page 99

5 **A** ▶ 4.4   **Pronunciation:** sentence stress   Listen to the sentences. Are the adverbs of frequency stressed or unstressed?

1 I usually get up at 7.00 a.m.
2 I always have a coffee for breakfast.

3 I never go to the gym.
4 I often make dinner in the evening.

B Listen again, check and repeat.

6 Change the adverbs of frequency in 5A so the sentences are true for you.
In pairs, say the sentences with the correct stress.

A *I sometimes get up at 7.00 a.m.*   **B** *Really? I never get up at 7.00 a.m.*

7 **A** Look at the table. Write five sentences about Sally and Ashley's brother, Marcus.

He always has breakfast in a café.

		Mon	Tue	Wed	Thu	Fri
1	have breakfast in a café	✔	✔	✔	✔	✔
2	watch TV in the morning	✔	✘	✔	✘	✔
3	work in the evening	✔	✘	✔	✔	✔
4	see friends after work	✘	✘	✘	✘	✔
5	go to bed before midnight	✘	✘	✘	✘	✘

B ▶ 4.5   Listen and check. What is Marcus's job?

Go to Communication practice: Student A page 136, Student B page 144

8 In pairs, compare yourself with members of your family. Use the activities in the boxes.

I always get up before 7.00 a.m., but my brother usually gets up late, at 9.30.

> get up before 7.00 a.m.   eat fast food   watch TV in the morning   go to bed late

> get home before 6.00 p.m.   have coffee for breakfast   have lunch at work   have a shower in the morning

---

Personal Best   Describe your typical daily routine at the weekend.

4B My journey to work

1 Match the types of transport with pictures a–e on page 35.

1 bike _____   4 car _____
2 taxi _____   5 subway _____
3 bus _____

Go to Vocabulary practice: transport, page 115

2 Look at the pictures and the title of the text on page 35. Guess the answers to the questions. Read the text quickly and check.

1 What city is it about?   2 What type of transport is it about?

> **Skill** | **finding specific information**
>
> **We sometimes need to find specific information in a text.**
> • Read the questions carefully to see what information you need to find.
> • Find the place in the text which has this information and read it carefully.
> • Don't worry if you don't understand every word.

3 A Read the Skill box. Then find information in the paragraph about Emily in the text to complete the first line of the table.

	Lives where?	Which job?	Works where?
Emily	*Harlem*		
Dan			
Megan			
Walter			

B Now find the information about the other people in the text. Complete the table.

4 Read the text again. Then in pairs, say why each person uses a *citibike*.

Emily uses a citibike because it's fast.

5 Complete the sentences from the text. In which sentences does *'s* mean *is*?

1 _____ office is in Downtown Manhattan.
2 'The _____ cheap,' she says.

> **Text builder** | **'s: possession or contraction**
>
> If you see *'s* at the end of a word, decide if it refers to possession or if it is a contraction of *is*.
> The **city's** blue public bikes = possession (the bikes belong to the city)
> **Megan's** a waitress in the Lower East Side = contraction (Megan is a waitress)

6 Read the Text builder. Then read the sentences and write *P* (possession) or *C* (contraction).

1 Ravi's a doctor. _____
2 David's mum is a teacher. _____
3 My train's always late. _____
4 Julia's brother starts work at 7.00. _____

7 Discuss the questions in pairs.

1 Do you have public bikes in your town or city? Are they popular? Why/Why not?
2 How do you usually travel to work or university?
3 Do you like the journey? Why/Why not?

A morning in the life of bike 0827

New York is famous for its yellow taxis and noisy subway, but a lot of people also travel by *citibike* – the city's blue public bikes. New Yorkers make 14 million journeys a year on *citibikes*. Who uses them and why? We follow one bike for a morning to find out.

7.15 a.m.
At Grand Central Station, Emily Adams from Harlem gets on bike number 0827. Emily's office is in Downtown Manhattan. She's a designer. Why does she use *citibike*? 'It's fast,' she says.

7.45 a.m.
Dan Pesci, an office worker, leaves his home in Soho. He gets on bike 0827 and goes to work in the Financial District. 'I usually go by subway', Dan says, 'but the weather's beautiful today.'

8.30 a.m.
Megan Chang from Brooklyn gets off the East River ferry. Megan's a waitress in the Lower East Side. 'The bike's cheap,' she says, 'but drivers in New York are crazy!'

9.30 a.m.
Doctor Walter Hart gets on bike 0827 and goes home to his apartment in Midtown. He works nights at a hospital on First Avenue. 'I like the exercise after work,' Walter says.

For bike 0827, it's sure to be a busy afternoon, evening and night.

4C Where do you work?

1 Match the adjectives in the box with their opposites.

quiet   clean   hot   fast   unfriendly

1 dirty / _____   **2** cold / _____   **3** friendly / _____   **4** noisy / _____   **5** slow / _____

Go to Vocabulary practice: adjectives (2), page 116

2 A Write down two examples for each of these things.

a cold country   a large building in your country   a noisy job   a long river   a fast animal

a friendly café or shop in your town or city   a hot drink   a quiet place in your town or city

B Compare your answers in pairs. Do you have the same things?

3 Read the text quickly and answer the questions.

1 What is Tess's job?   _____   **3** What time does she start work?   _____

2 Does she like her job?   _____   **4** Where does she live?   _____

A Dirty Job?

Tess Mitchell is a refuse collector. It's dirty work and she gets up very early, but she loves her job.

What time do you start work?

I start work at 5.00 in the morning. I get up at 4.15 a.m. and have breakfast. Then I leave for work.

¹_____ do you work?

I work in south London. The refuse centre isn't far from my house.

²_____ do you do on a typical day?

I drive the lorry to about 800 houses every day from Monday to Friday. That's a lot of rubbish!

³_____ do you like the job?

Because the people are friendly and I work outside. Sometimes it's very cold early in the morning, but when the weather's nice, I love it.

⁴_____ do you finish work?

I finish at 1.30 p.m. I'm a mum, so the hours are great. I get home at 2.00, have a shower, and then I go to my children's school to collect them.

⁵_____ do you relax when you're not at work?

I play football with a women's football team and we train on Tuesday and Thursday evenings. At the weekend, I get up late!

4 A Complete the questions in the text with the question words in the box. How do you say them in your language?

> Why   Where   When   What   How

B Look at the questions in the text again. Order the words below from 1–4 to make a question. Then read the Grammar box.

☐ *do/does*   ☐ main verb   ☐ question word   ☐ subject

📖 **Grammar**   **present simple: *wh-* questions**

Question word:	*do/does*:	Subject:	Main verb:
Where	*do*	*you*	*live?*
What	*does*	*your husband*	*do?*
How	*does*	*he*	*get to work?*
When	*do*	*your children*	*watch TV?*
What time	*do*	*they*	*get up?*
Why	*do*	*you*	*work at the weekend?*
Who	*do*	*you*	*work with?*

Go to Grammar practice: present simple: *wh-* questions, page 99

5 ▶ **4.10**   **Pronunciation:** question words   Listen and repeat the question words. Do they begin with a /w/ sound or a /h/ sound?

1 where _____   **2** when _____   **3** who _____   **4** why _____   **5** how _____   **6** what _____

6 A ▶ **4.11**   Order the words to make questions. Say the questions with the correct pronunciation of the question words. Listen, check and repeat.

1 you / have / how many / do / children   _____ ?
2 what / they / time / have breakfast / do   _____ ?
3 do / does / husband / your / what   _____ ?
4 he / when / does / work   _____ ?
5 at the weekend / you / what / do / do   _____ ?

B ▶ **4.12**   Match questions 1–5 with answers a–e. Listen to the interview with Tess and check.

a In the afternoons and evenings.
b Two.
c He's a taxi driver.
d 7.30.
e We often go to the park.

Go to Communication practice: Student A page 137, Student B page 145

7 A Find out about your partner. Ask and answer the questions in the boxes in pairs.

> What time / start work?
> Who / live with?
> How / get to English classes?

> What / have for breakfast?
> Where / usually go on holiday?
> How / relax in the evening?

> Why / study English?
> When / do your English homework?
> How many brothers and sisters / have?

B Swap partners. Ask and answer questions about your first partner.

A *What time does Sasha start work?*   **B** *He usually starts work at 8.00 a.m.*

Personal Best   Write ten questions for an interview with an actor/singer that you like.

4D How can I help you?

1 A ▶ 4.13 Match the prices with the words. Listen and check.

a £5
b $50
c €15
d £5.95
e 50p
f 50c
g £19.99
h €9.99
i $25
j $11.99
k £6.50
l €29

1 nine euros ninety-nine	_____	7 fifty pence/fifty p _____
2 nineteen pounds ninety-nine	_____	8 five pounds _____
3 fifteen euros	_____	9 six pounds fifty _____
4 fifty dollars	_____	10 fifty cents _____
5 eleven dollars ninety-nine	_____	11 five pounds ninety-five _____
6 twenty-nine euros	_____	12 twenty-five dollars _____

B Write down three prices in numbers and give them to your partner. Say your partner's prices.

That's three pounds fifty.

2 Discuss the questions in pairs.

1 Who usually goes shopping for food in your house?
2 Where do you usually buy food? Why?
   a at a supermarket   **b** at a market   **c** at local shops
3 Do you like shopping for food? Why/Why not?

Penny

3 ▶ 4.14 Watch or listen to the first part of *Learning Curve*. Are the sentences true (T) or false (F)?

1 Penny likes shopping for food. _____
2 Penny and Taylor live together. _____
3 They usually go shopping on Thursdays. _____
4 There is a big supermarket near their apartment. _____

4 ▶ 4.15 Watch or listen to the second part of the show. Tick (✔) the things Penny buys and the correct prices.

shop 1 | shop 2 | shop 3

half a chicken ☐	cheese and salad ☐	a blue shopping trolley ☐
a whole chicken ☐	cheese and eggs ☐	a black shopping trolley ☐
$4.79 ☐	$17.15 ☐	$21.77 ☐
$8.79 ☐	$17.50 ☐	$22.02 ☐

5 ▶ 4.15 Who says the phrases: Penny (P), Shop assistant 1 (S1), Shop assistant 2 (S2) or Shop assistant 3 (S3)? Watch or listen again and check.

1 How much is it for that small shopping trolley? _____
2 Here you are. _____
3 I'd like a whole chicken, please. _____
4 You're welcome. _____
5 Here's your change – 25 cents. _____
6 Can I have two pounds of this white cheese? _____

Conversation builder **shopping for food**

Customer:
Do you have ...?
Can I have ...
I'd like ...
How much is that?
Here you go/are.

Shop assistant:
How can I help you?
Anything else?
That's ... dollars/pounds.
Here you go/are.
Here's your change.

6 A Read the Conversation builder. Then order the sentences from 1–7 to make a conversation in a shop.

a ☐ Yes. Anything else?
b ☐ Yes, I'd like five biscuits, please. How much is that?
c ☐ Can I have a chocolate cake, please?
d ☐ Thanks. And here's your change.
e ☐ Here you go – £10.
f ☐ Hello. How can I help you?
g ☐ That's £8.50.

B ▶ 4.16 Listen and check. Practise the conversation in pairs.

7 ▶ 4.17 Complete the conversation with the words in the box. Listen and check. Are Penny and the shop assistant polite? Why/Why not?

welcome   good   thank you   please

Shop assistant ¹_____ evening.	**Penny** ³_____ .
Penny I'd like a whole chicken, ²_____ .	**Shop assistant** You're ⁴_____ .
Shop assistant Here you go.	

Skill **being polite in shops**

It's important to be polite if you work in a shop or if you're a customer.
• Greet people. Say: *Hi / Good morning / Good evening*, etc.
• Ask for things politely. Say: *Can I have ...? / I'd like ..., please.* NOT ~~I want ... / Give me ...~~
• If someone says: *Thanks / Thank you*, you can reply: *You're welcome. / That's alright.*

8 ▶ 4.18 Read the Skill box. Listen to three conversations. Tick (✔) the people who are polite.
1 a the customer ☐ **b** the waiter ☐ **c** both people ☐
2 a the customer ☐ **b** the shop assistant ☐ **c** both people ☐
3 a the customer ☐ **b** the receptionist ☐ **c** both people ☐

Go to Communication practice: Student A page 137, Student B page 145

9 A PREPARE In pairs, look at the pictures and choose one of the situations. Write down things you can buy there and their prices.

In a burger restaurant

In a fruit and vegetable shop

In a café

B PRACTISE Decide who is the customer and who is the assistant. Act out your conversation.

C PERSONAL BEST Listen to another pair's conversation. Are they polite? What could they do better?

Personal Best   Think of your favourite food shop or café and write a conversation in English there.

Grammar

1 Tick (✔) the correct sentences.

1   a   I never finish work at 5.00 p.m. ☐
    b   I don't never finish work at 5.00 p.m. ☐
    c   I don't finish work never at 5.00 p.m. ☐

2   a   He don't go to bed early. ☐
    b   He not go to bed early. ☐
    c   He doesn't go to bed early. ☐

3   a   Do you go to work by car? ☐
    b   Does you go to work by car? ☐
    c   When you do go to work by car? ☐

4   a   We often has eggs for breakfast. ☐
    b   We often have eggs for breakfast. ☐
    c   We have often eggs for breakfast. ☐

5   a   Why do you live with? ☐
    b   Who do you live with? ☐
    c   How do you live with? ☐

6   a   When they do get up? ☐
    b   When they get up? ☐
    c   When do they get up? ☐

7   a   She work in a restaurant in the evening. ☐
    b   She do work in a restaurant in the evening. ☐
    c   She works in a restaurant in the evening. ☐

8   a   Goes he to the gym after work? ☐
    b   Does he to the gym after work? ☐
    c   Does he go to the gym after work? ☐

2 Order the words to make questions and sentences.

1   your / do / go / children / where / school / to
    _____ ?

2   have / she / at / does / lunch / home
    _____ ?

3   always / dinner / we / eat / vegetables / for
    _____ .

4   get / time / what / weekend / do / up / the / you / at
    _____ ?

5   don't / shopping / I / Saturday / go / on
    _____ .

6   the / he / book / sometimes / a / reads / train / on
    _____ .

7   Monday / quiet / restaurant / is / on / often / the
    _____ .

8   in / radio / do / listen / to / you / the / morning / the
    _____ ?

9   old / brother's / is / how / your / girlfriend
    _____ ?

10 the / never / exercise / Simon / weekend / does / at
    _____ .

3 Complete the text with the correct form of the verbs in brackets.

Life on Muck

 This is Laura Marriner. She lives and works on the very small island of Muck in Scotland. Life isn't easy, but it's very interesting …

What ¹_____ (be) **Laura's job?**
She's a teacher. Her school only ²_____ (have) eight children.

Where ³_____ **she** _____ (live)?
Laura ⁴ _____ (not leave) home in the morning because she lives in the school with her husband and two sons!

How ⁵_____ **they** _____ (go) **shopping?**
By ferry. The journey is two hours, but people on the island only ⁶_____ (use) the ferry when the weather is good. They ⁷_____ (not go) shopping every day, so Laura ⁸_____ (make) bread at home.

What is school life like on Muck?
It's great. The children often ⁹_____ (study) on the beach.

¹⁰_____ **Laura** _____ (like) **life on Muck?**
Yes, she does! When the weather is horrible, life is difficult, but she's happy there. The people are very friendly and life is an adventure.

Vocabulary

1 Put the words in the box in the correct columns.

~~boat~~ ~~cold~~ ~~do~~ cheese fast finish get up
know small meat noisy short taxi train want

Verbs	Adjectives	Nouns
do	*cold*	*boat*

2 Circle the word that is different. Explain your answers.

1	car	lorry	bus	plane
2	think	use	slow	make
3	Friday	tomorrow	Sunday	Saturday
4	rice	chips	crisps	potatoes
5	coffee	milk	fruit	orange juice
6	clean	horrible	unfriendly	dirty
7	biscuit	pizza	cake	chocolate
8	work	study	change	dinner

3 Complete the sentences with the correct words.

1 What time do you g_et_ home after work?

2 He usually l_____ to the radio at work.

3 I always have b_____ before I leave home in the morning.

4 They w_____ television after dinner.

5 She goes to university by m_____ . It's very fast.

6 In cold weather, I have a h_____ drink in the evening.

7 He never says 'hello'. He's so u_____ .

8 T_____ in New York are yellow and in London they're black.

9 I never drink tea, coffee or soft drinks. I only drink w_____ with meals.

10 On W_____ evening, I go to the gym.

4 Complete the email with the words in the box.

> bike   dressed   bread   friendly   get   live
> go   evening   Saturday   read

Hi Ana,

How are you? I'm in Cartagena at my grandmother's house this week. It's nice and quiet here. I ¹_____ up late every day, have breakfast and get ²_____ . Then I go to the shops by ³_____ . I usually buy some ⁴_____ for lunch. The people are very ⁵_____ . In the afternoon, I ⁶_____ to the beach and ⁷_____ a book. In the ⁸_____ , we sometimes have dinner in a restaurant.

I'm here for one week, and then I go home on ⁹_____ ☹ … I want to ¹⁰_____ here!

See you soon.

Bea

Personal Best

Lesson 3A
Name four things people eat or drink for breakfast.

Lesson 4A
Write four sentences about your daily routine with adverbs of frequency.

Lesson 3A
Write a sentence about the food you like and don't like.

Lesson 4B
Name six types of transport.

Lesson 3B
Name the days of the week that begin with 'T'.

Lesson 4B
Describe a member of your family's bike, car or motorbike.

Lesson 3B
Write a sentence about something you do every week.

Lesson 4C
Write three adjectives that describe your town or city.

Lesson 3C
Write a positive and a negative sentence about a friend's typical day.

Lesson 4C
Write three questions for your teacher with different question words.

Lesson 3D
Write about the food you eat on a special occasion. Use *and* and *but*.

Lesson 4D
Write a sentence to ask for something to eat and drink in a café.

All about me

5A When can you start?

1 Complete phrases 1–5 with the verbs in the box.

swim speak drive play call

1 _____ a car   2 _____ Chinese   3 _____ the piano   4 _____ a friend   5 _____ in the sea

Go to Vocabulary practice: common verbs (2), page 117

2 Read the job advert. What do you need for this job?

JOBS TO GO.COM

▶ FIND JOBS
▶ POST CV
▶ COMPANY PROFILES

SYDNEY CITY TOURS: TOUR GUIDE

Help tourists see the beautiful city of Sydney.

Do you know Sydney? Do you like working with people? Can you speak a foreign language? Do you want to work this summer?

If the answer is 'Yes', then contact us.

▶ CONTACT

3 ▶ 5.2 Listen to a job interview. Tick (✔) the things Georgia can do. Does she get the job?

	Yes	No
1 Can you speak a foreign language?		
2 Can you drive?		
3 Can you work early in the morning?		
4 Can you swim well?		

4 **A** ▶ 5.2 Match the halves to make sentences. Listen again and check.

1 Some of the people can't
2 I can speak
3 Yes, I
4 No, I
5 When can you

a can.
b start?
c Chinese.
d can't – sorry.
e speak English.

B Choose the correct options to complete the rules.
Then read the Grammar box.

1 We use *can* to talk about *abilities / daily routines*.
2 We use *can't* + verb in *questions / negatives*.
3 We use *can* + subject + verb in *questions / negatives*.

Grammar   *can* and *can't*

Positive:	Negative:	Questions and short answers:
I **can work** this summer.	I **can't speak** Chinese.	**Can** you **speak** a foreign language?
Georgia **can swim** well.	They **can't cook**.	Yes, I **can**. No, I **can't**.

Personal Best

Go to Grammar practice: *can* and *can't*, page 100

5 ▶5.4 **Pronunciation:** *can* and *can't* Listen and repeat. Pay attention to the difference between *can* /kæn/ or /kən/ and *can't* /kɑːnt/.

1 He can drive.   **2** She can't swim.   **3** Can you play the guitar?   **4** Yes, I can.

6 A ▶5.5 Say the sentences with the correct pronunciation of *can* and *can't*. Listen, check and repeat.

1 I can swim two kilometres.   **3** I can't speak German.   **5** I can drive a car.
2 I can't sing well.   **4** I can cook Italian food.   **6** I can't play the piano.

B Say the sentences in pairs. Say if you think it's true or false for your partner.

A *I can swim two kilometres.*   **B** *False. You can't swim two kilometres.*
A *You're right, I can't swim.*

7 A Read the job advert. What does an *au pair* do?

B ▶5.6 Emily and Ben are interested in the job. Listen and tick (✔) what they can and can't do.

AU PAIR

- **Can you look after children?**
- **Do you like sports and music?**
- **Do you want to work as an au pair this summer?**

We're a friendly American family with two children. We live in Madrid, Spain.

– *Contact Lisa Jones for more information.* –

Can he/she ...	Emily	Ben
cook?		
drive?		
speak Spanish?		
play tennis?		
swim?		
play the piano?		
play the guitar?		
sing?		

8 ▶5.7 In pairs, ask and answer the questions about Emily and Ben. Who is best for the job? Listen and check.

A *Can Emily cook?*   **B** *Yes, she can.*

Go to Communication practice: Student A page 137, Student B page 145

9 A Ask your classmates questions 1–5. Find someone who says 'Yes, I can.' and write his/her name. Then ask for more information.

A *Can you speak a foreign language?*   **B** *Yes, I can.*
A *Which language can you speak?*   **B** *I can speak French.*

Questions	Name	More information
1 Can you speak a foreign language?		
2 Can you play an instrument?		
3 Can you dance?		
4 Can you cook?		
5 Can you play a sport?		

B In pairs, discuss what you found out about your classmates.

Sebastian can speak French.

Personal Best Write ten sentences about people in your class. Use *can* and *can't*.

Learning Curve

5B I can't live without my phone

1 Match the words in the box with the electronic devices 1–6. Is your family like this?

> headphones   laptop   smartphone   MP3 player   TV   remote control

1 _____ 2 _____ 3 _____ 4 _____ 5 _____ 6 _____

Personal Best

Go to Vocabulary practice: electronic devices, page 118

2 Which electronic devices do you have? Discuss in pairs.
I have a laptop, but I don't have a tablet.

3 ▶ 5.9 Watch or listen to the first part of *Learning Curve*. Tick (✔) the devices Kate mentions.
camera ☐   desktop computer ☐   TV ☐   smartphone ☐   laptop ☐   headphones ☐

🔧 **Skill**   **listening for specific information**

We sometimes need to listen for specific information.
- Read the questions to find out what information you need.
- Think about the topic and what type of information it is, e.g. a person, a place, a number, etc.
- Listen carefully when the speakers talk about this topic.

---

4 ▶ 5.9 Read the Skill box. Watch or listen again and choose the correct options to answer the questions.

1 Which sport does Kate do on Friday?
  a basketball   **b** football   **c** tennis
2 What language does she learn on her tablet and phone?
  a Spanish   **b** French   **c** Italian
3 What device can't she live without?
  a tablet   **b** camera   **c** phone
4 How many photos do people take every year?
  a one million   **b** one billion   **c** one trillion
5 How many televisions do people in the USA have?
  a 116 million   **b** 123 million   **c** 26 million

5 ▶ 5.10   Watch or listen to the rest of the show. Complete the sentences with the words in the box.

> headphones   DVR   car   laptop   tablet   music

Simon

Parminder

Vincent

1 Simon can't live without _____ or his _____ .

2 Parminder can't live without her _____ and _____ .

3 Vincent can't live without his _____ and his _____ .

6 ▶ 5.10   Watch or listen again. Choose the correct options to complete the sentences.

1 Parminder uses her devices for *presentations / letters / games*.

2 She uses her devices *at the weekend / at night / every day*.

3 Vincent can play *the piano / the violin / the guitar*.

4 His car is from *1962 / 1967 / 1972*.

5 Simon travels *by underground / on foot / by car*.

7 ▶ 5.11   Listen to Vincent's sentence. Is it easy to hear the <u>underlined</u> words? Why?

> And when I <u>get</u> <u>home</u>, I <u>watch</u> <u>TV</u> at <u>night</u>.

◄◄◄ Listening builder   sentence stress

In English, we stress the important words in sentences. You can usually understand the general idea if you only hear these words.
I <u>play</u> <u>basketball</u> on <u>Fridays</u> with a <u>women's</u> <u>team</u>.
I <u>work</u> for a <u>big</u> <u>company</u> and we <u>use</u> <u>all</u> the <u>top</u> <u>technology</u>.

8 A ▶ 5.12   Read the Listening builder. Read and listen to sentences 1–4. Can you understand them?

1 _____ can't live without _____ phone. _____ _____ call people _____ take photos.

2 _____ brother's _____ doctor. _____ usually goes _____ _____ hospital _____ car.

3 Kevin wants _____ new laptop, _____ _____ very expensive.

4 _____ _____ morning, _____ always listen _____ _____ radio.

B ▶ 5.12   Listen again and complete the sentences with the unstressed words.

9 In pairs, talk about your electronic devices. Answer the questions.

1 What do you use your devices for?

2 Which device can't you live without? Why not?

A *I use my phone to listen to music and take photos. What about you?*

B *I don't use my phone to listen to music. I have an MP3 player.*

Personal Best   Write about your favourite electronic device. Say when and where you use it.

5C I love it!

1 Match the words in the box with pictures a–f.

cycling   walking   cleaning   swimming   reading   cooking

Go to Vocabulary practice: activities, page 119

2 A Write two activities in each column.

😊 I love …	🙂 I like …	☹️ I don't like …	😣 I hate …

B Tell your partner about what you love, like, don't like and hate.

A *I love cooking.*   **B** *Really? I hate cooking. I love going out!*

3 A Look at the pictures on the webpage. What activities can you see?

B Read the text. Complete the sentences with *loves*, *likes*, *doesn't like* and *hates*.

1 Midori _____ listening to music. She _____ Adele.
2 Laura _____ shopping for food.
3 Diego _____ his grandad.
4 Josh _____ sleeping late because he _____ early mornings.
5 Ellie _____ watching movies with her friends and she _____ popcorn.

That's ⓘnteresting   **LIKES** AND **DISLIKES**

I like listening to music. Adele is my favourite singer. I love her!

♥ 4   **Midori**

I like watching movies with my friends. We always have a big bowl of popcorn – I love it!

♥ 6   **Ellie**

My brother and I don't like shopping for food. Mum always takes us at the weekend!

♥ 7   **Laura**

I love my grandad. I can always talk to him and he helps me a lot.

♥ 12   **Diego**

I love sleeping late at weekends. Early mornings? I hate them!

♥ 3   **Josh**

4 A Match the object pronouns in **bold** with the people and things. Read the text again and check.

1 I love **her**!
2 Mum always takes **us** at the weekend!
3 I can always talk to **him**.
4 He helps **me** a lot.
5 I hate **them**!
6 I love **it**!

a Diego
b early mornings
c Adele
d popcorn
e Laura and her brother
f Diego's grandad

B Choose the correct words to complete the sentences. Then read the Grammar box.

1 We use object pronouns instead of *people and things / times and places.*
2 We use object pronouns *before / after* verbs.

📖 **Grammar object pronouns**

Subject pronouns:	Object pronouns:	
I	me	*I don't understand. Can you help **me**?*
you	you	*Are **you** Adam? This is for **you**.*
he	him	***He** isn't friendly. I don't like **him**.*
she	her	***She** works in your office. Do you know **her**?*
it	it	***It**'s perfect. I love **it**!*
we	us	***We**'re in the garden. Can you see **us**?*
they	them	***They**'re new here. I don't know **them**.*

Go to Grammar practice: object pronouns, page 100

5 A ▶5.15 **Pronunciation:** /h/ Listen and repeat. Pay attention to the sound /h/.

him   her   he   help   happy

B ▶5.16 Say the questions and sentences. Then listen, check and repeat.

1 Do you like him?   2 I can't see her.   3 He hates horses.   4 Hi, Harry. How are you?

6 ▶5.17 Complete the conversation with object pronouns. Listen and check.

A Do you like Emma Stone?
B Yes, I do. I love ¹_____ . She's great!
A What about Bruno Mars?
B Yes, I like ²_____ too.
A Do you like shopping for clothes?

B No, I hate ³_____ .
A Do you like Monday mornings?
B No, I hate ⁴_____ .
A What do you think of cats?
B I don't like ⁵_____ , but they like ⁶_____ !

Go to Communication practice: Student A page 138, Student B page 146

7 A Write three examples in each of the circles.

singers and bands	actors	food and drink	animals	activities

B In pairs, ask and answer questions about the people and things.

Do you like …?   What about …?   What do you think of …?

8 Tell the class about you and your partner.

We both love cats. I like Ryan Gosling, but Carla doesn't like him.

Personal Best Write a conversation like the one in exercise 6 between you and someone in your family.

5D My profile

1 A Look at the profile on the 'CityMeet' app. What do you think you can do with the app?

a find an apartment in a city   b make new friends in a city   c find a new job in a city

B Read the profile and check.

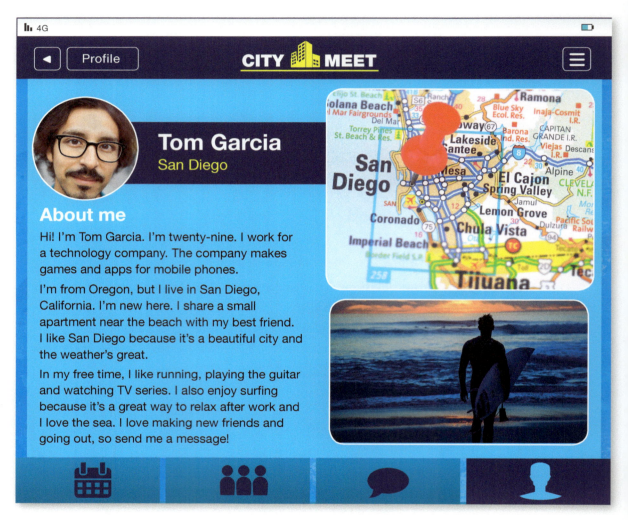

2 Read the profile again. Complete the sentences with the correct words.

1 Tom works for a _____ company.
2 He's from _____ , but he lives in _____ .
3 He lives near the _____ with his _____ .
4 He thinks the weather in San Diego is _____ .

5 He plays the _____ and watches _____ in his free time.
6 He loves making _____ .

 **Skill** describing yourself

When you write a text to describe yourself, use a different paragraph for each topic.

- personal information about you and your job: *Hi! My name's Fiona. I'm a teacher.*
- where you live: *I live in York. I share a flat with my best friend.*
- what you do in your free time: *In my free time, I like listening to music and cooking for friends.*
- information about your family: *I have a brother. His name's Paul and he's 18.*

3 Read the Skill box. Tick (✔) the topics which are in Tom's profile.

a his job ☐   b where he lives ☐   c his family ☐   d his free-time activities ☐

4 Complete Kimberley's profile with sentences a–c.

   a I also love travelling because it's a great way to meet new people.

   b I study French and Spanish. I can also speak Portuguese.

   c We love San Diego because it's a fun and exciting city.

ABOUT ME

Hello! I'm Kimberley Watson and I'm a student at the University of San Diego. ¹____

I live in a house with four friends. We're all students. ²____

In my free time, I like watching French films, running and going out with my friends. ³____

5 Imagine Tom and Kimberley meet on CityMeet. Do they become friends? Choose an option and complete the sentence.

Tom and Kimberley *become / don't become* friends because _____ .

⟷ **Text builder**   *because*

We use *because* to give a reason. It answers the question *Why?*
*I like San Diego **because** it's a beautiful city.*
Why do you like travelling?   ***Because** it's a great way to meet new people.*

---

6 A Read the Text builder and find sentences with *because* in Tom and Kimberley's profiles. How do you say *because* in your language?

  B Match 1–5 with a–e. Make sentences with *because*.

1	I live in a small flat	**a**	I'm usually tired after work.
2	I go to work by bus	**b**	it's good exercise.
3	I like swimming	**c**	it's quiet and the people are friendly.
4	I don't often go to the gym	**d**	houses in my city are expensive.
5	I like living in a village	**e**	I can't drive.

7 Complete the sentences with your own ideas.

  1 I love my city/town because _____ .

  2 I'm often tired in the evening because _____ .

  3 I like cooking because _____ .

  4 I don't often go out because _____ .

  5 I usually get up early because _____ .

8 A **PREPARE** Plan an online profile for you. Decide what information to include. Make notes about:

  • your personal information

  • your work or study

  • where you live and who you live with

  • your free-time activities and why you like them

  B **PRACTISE** Write your profile. Use one paragraph for each topic. Remember to use *because* to give reasons.

  C **PERSONAL BEST** Read your partner's profile. Does each paragraph contain one topic? Choose a paragraph that you like and tell your partner why you like it.

Personal Best   Write a profile of a friend or someone in your family.

Hello The verb *be* (*I, you*)

We use the verb *be* to give information about people.

I'm Carlos and I'm a teacher.

We usually use contractions in positive and negative forms.

You're a student. = You are a student.
I'm not in Class 3. = I am not in Class 3.

▶ 1.4	I	you
+	I**'m** a student.	You**'re** a teacher.
−	I**'m not** a teacher.	You **aren't** a student.
?	**Am** I in Class 2?	**Are** you in my class?
Y/N	Yes, I **am**. / No, I**'m not**.	Yes, you **are**. / No, you **aren't**.

1 Choose the correct words to complete the sentences and questions.

1 I *'m* / *'re* Harry.
2 You *'m* / *'re* Lola.
3 *Am* / *Are* you a student?
4 *Am I* / *I'm* in Room 3.
5 *Are you* / *You are* late?
6 No, I *'m not* / *aren't*.
7 *Am* / *Are* I in this class?
8 Yes, you *am* / *are*.

◀ Go back to page 4

1A The verb *be* (*he, she, it*)

We use *he*, *she* and *it* to talk about a person or a thing.

The teacher is Mexican. He's from Puebla.
The car isn't from Germany. It's from Japan.

We usually use contractions in positive and negative forms.

Akemi isn't Chinese. = Akemi is not Chinese.
She's Japanese. = She is Japanese.

▶ 1.14	he	she	it
+	Leo**'s** from Peru.	Lucía**'s** Colombian.	The book**'s** Chinese.
−	He **isn't** from Chile.	She **isn't** Argentinian.	It **isn't** Italian.
?	**Is** Ravi from India?	**Is** Ayla Turkish?	**Is** the car German?
Y/N	Yes, he **is**. / No, he **isn't**.	Yes, she **is**. / No, she **isn't**.	Yes, it **is**. / No, it **isn't**.

1 Complete the sentences with the correct words.

1 This is my friend Daniel. He _____ from Spain.
2 Anna isn't in class today. _____'s at home.
3 Sophie _____ a student. She's the teacher.
4 This is my car. _____'s a Toyota.
5 A Where _____ Leonardo DiCaprio from?
  B He _____ from the USA.
6 A What's the capital of Australia? Is _____ Sydney?
  B No, it _____ . It's Canberra.
7 A _____ María from Colombia?
  B No, she _____ . She's from Mexico.
8 A Is sushi from Japan?
  B Yes, _____ is.

◀ Go back to page 7

1C The verb *be* (*we, you, they*)

We use *we*, *you* and *they* to talk about people and things in the plural.

The engineers are here. They're from India.
Susan and I aren't happy. We're sad.

We usually use contractions in positive and negative forms.

You're in Class 3. = You are in Class 3.
The pizzas aren't expensive. = The pizzas are not expensive.

▶ 1.29	we	you	they
+	We**'re** 25 years old.	You**'re** doctors.	They**'re** French.
−	We **aren't** old.	You **aren't** chefs.	Ana and Bea **aren't** here.
?	**Are** we sad?	**Are** you happy?	**Are** they in Class 4?
Y/N	Yes, we **are**. / No, we **aren't**.	Yes, you **are**. / No, you **aren't**.	Yes, they **are**. / No, they **aren't**.

1 Rewrite the sentences. Change the words in **bold** to *we*, *you* or *they*.

1 **Elsa and Lucy** are police officers.
   _____

2 **Maite and I** are 21 years old.
   _____

3 Are **you and Wei** from China?
   _____

4 **The doctors** aren't from India.
   _____

5 Where are **Maggie and Jake Gyllenhaal** from?
   _____

6 How old are **you and your friend**?
   _____

2 Choose the correct words to complete the questions and sentences.

1 We *isn't* / *aren't* doctors.
2 *Is* / *Are* Ismail from Turkey?
3 Sam and I *am* / *are* in London.
4 I *'m not* / *aren't* your teacher.
5 Where *is* / *are* the actor from?
6 Ana and Rosa *is* / *are* from Spain.

◀ Go back to page 11

2A Singular and plural nouns

We use *a* and *an* with singular nouns. We use *a* with nouns that start with consonants (*b*, *d*, *f*, *g*, etc.) and we use *an* with nouns that start with vowels (*a*, *e*, *i*, *o*, *u*).

It's a book.   She's an actor.

To make a noun plural, we usually add *-s* or *-es*.

a key ⇒ three keys   a watch ⇒ two watches

▶ 2.3	Singular	Plural
	It's **an** umbrella.	They're umbrella**s**.
	I'm **a** waitress.	We're waitress**es**.

Spelling rules for plurals
We usually add *-s* to nouns to make a plural.
bag ⇒ bags
When a noun ends in a consonant + *y*, we remove the *y* and then add *-ies*.
country ⇒ countries
When a noun ends in *ch*, *sh*, *s* or *x*, we add *-es*.
watch ⇒ watches
Some plurals are irregular.
child ⇒ children   man ⇒ men   woman ⇒ women   person ⇒ people

2A *this, that, these, those*

We use *this* and *these* + the verb *be* to identify things that are near us.

This is my bag and these are my sunglasses.

We use *that* and *those* + the verb *be* to identify things that aren't near us.

That's my school and those are my friends.

▶ 2.4	Things that are near	Things that aren't near
Singular	**This** is my wallet.	**That**'s my teacher.
Plural	**These** are my books.	**Those** are my classmates.

> **Look!** We can also use *this/that/these/those* + noun. *That book is new.*

2C Possessive adjectives, *'s* for possession

We use possessive adjectives before nouns to say that something belongs to someone.

Joseph is my brother.   This is our house.

We use the same possessive adjectives for singular and plural nouns.

Is that your key?   Are those your keys?

▶ 2.11	Possessive adjectives
my	I'm French. **My** wife is Spanish.
your	Are **you** sad? **Your** boyfriend isn't here.
his	**He**'s a teacher. **His** students are young.
her	**She**'s an actor. **Her** house is big.
its	**It**'s a small restaurant. **Its** pizzas are good.
our	**We**'re late. **Our** boss isn't happy.
their	**They**'re tour guides. **Their** jobs are interesting.

If we talk about possession with a name or a noun, we add *'s* to the name or noun.

Is that the teacher's book?   Are you Rob's sister?

---

1 Complete the sentences with singular or plural nouns and *a* or *an*, if necessary.

Singular	Plural
1 It's a city.	They're _____ .
2 She's _____ .	They're actors.
3 Are you a waitress?	Are you _____ ?
4 He isn't _____ .	They aren't children.
5 It's a watch.	They're _____ .
6 It isn't _____ .	They aren't umbrellas.
7 I'm a woman.	We're _____ .
8 He's _____ .	They're people.

2 Match the parts to make sentences and questions.

1 Alice is an _____	**a** tour guide.
2 It's an _____	**b** IT worker.
3 He's a _____	**c** umbrella.
4 Jo and I are _____	**d** engineers.
5 Are you a _____	**e** sunglasses?
6 Where are my _____	**f** chef?

◀ Go back to page 14

1 Choose the correct words to complete the sentences.

1 *This / These* is my room.
2 Excuse me. Are *that / those* your glasses?
3 Look! Is *this / that* your phone over there?
4 Are *these / this* your keys?
5 Is *that / those* your pen, or is it my pen?
6 Are *these / this* your credit cards?

◀ Go back to page 15

1 Complete the sentences with the correct possessive adjectives.

1 Hello. _____ name's Kate.
2 We're from Lima. This is a photo of _____ house.
3 He's French. _____ name is Olivier.
4 They're British, but _____ parents are from Peru.
5 Hi, I'm Tom. What's _____ name?
6 This is Luisa and _____ husband, Sven.

2 Complete the sentences with *'s* for possession so they mean the same as the first sentences.

1 She's Olivia. Those are her sunglasses.
Those are <u>Olivia's sunglasses</u> .
2 He's my son. That's his credit card.
That's _____ .
3 This is my daughter. Her name is Ruby.
My _____ .
4 She's our doctor. Her phone number is 665342.
Our _____ .

◀ Go back to page 19

3A Present simple (*I, you, we, they*)

We use the present simple to talk about facts and routines.

I drink coffee for breakfast.
We eat a lot of fruit.

We form negatives with *don't* (*do not*) + the infinitive of the verb.

My parents don't like tea.
They don't eat meat.

We form questions with *do* + subject + the infinitive of the verb.

Do you like fish?
Do they have breakfast?

▶ 3.3	I / you / we / they
+	I **have** a big breakfast. You **eat** a lot of fruit.
–	We **don't drink** coffee. They **don't like** cheese.
?	**Do** you **have** a big breakfast? **Do** they **eat** fish?
Y/N	Yes, I **do**. / No, I **don't**. Yes, they **do**. / No, they **don't**.

1 Complete the sentences with the correct form of the verbs in brackets.

1 I _____ pizza. (like)
2 We _____ eggs or cheese. (not eat)
3 They _____ lunch at home. (not have)
4 You _____ tea. (drink)
5 Our children _____ green vegetables. (not like)
6 My husband and I _____ a lot of fruit. (eat)
7 I _____ coffee at night. (not drink)
8 You _____ breakfast. (not have)

2 Order the words to make questions. Then complete the short answers.

1 you / meat / eat / do
_____ ? No, I _____ .
2 you / do / food / like / Indian
_____ ? Yes, we _____ .
3 potatoes / they / like / do
_____ ? Yes, they _____ .
4 drink / do / you and Anna / coffee
_____ ? No, we _____ .

◀ Go back to page 25

3C Present simple (*he, she, it*)

For *he, she* and *it*, we often add -*s* to the infinitive to make the positive form.

I drink tea for breakfast. ⇨ *He drinks tea for breakfast.*

Spelling rules for present simple verbs with *he, she, it*
We usually add -*s* to the infinitive. *work* ⇨ *works*
When a verb ends in a consonant + *y*, we remove the *y* and then add -*ies*. *study* ⇨ *studies*
When a verb ends in **ch**, **sh**, **s** or **x**, we add -*es*. *watch* ⇨ *watches*
Some verbs are irregular. *go* ⇨ *goes*   *do* ⇨ *does*   *have* ⇨ *has*

We form negatives with *doesn't* (*does not*) + the infinitive of the verb.

My sister doesn't speak English.

We form questions with *does* + subject + the infinitive of the verb.

Does our teacher work at the weekend?

▶ 3.14	he / she / it
+	Kevin **does** exercise in the morning. She **lives** in Scotland.
–	He **doesn't want** a new car. My house **doesn't have** a garden.
?	**Does** he **live** in London? **Does** Sandra **go** to the gym?
Y/N	Yes, he **does**. / No, he **doesn't**. Yes, she **does**. / No, she **doesn't**.

1 Write the present simple *he, she, it* form of the verbs.

1 like _____
2 have _____
3 play _____
4 eat _____
5 go _____
6 try _____
7 drink _____
8 wash _____

2 Rewrite the sentences. Use positive (+), negative (–) or question (?) forms.

1 My father makes good cakes.
_____ (?)
2 Anna doesn't study at university.
_____ (+)
3 Mark works on Tuesday.
_____ (–)
4 Does she have two children?
_____ (+)
5 Sam thinks about football all day.
_____ (?)
6 My sister doesn't watch TV in the evening.
_____ (+)

◀ Go back to page 29

4A Adverbs of frequency

We use adverbs of frequency with the present simple to talk about routines.

They always go to the gym on Friday.
I sometimes play football at the weekend.

Adverbs of frequency come before most verbs, but we put adverbs of frequency after the verb *be*.

I usually have lunch at work.
I'm always at home in the evening. **NOT** *I always am at home in the evening.*

▶ 4.3	Adverbs of frequency	
always	He **always** has a shower in the morning.	100%
usually	Julia **usually** gets up early.	
often	You **often** get home after 9.00 p.m.	
sometimes	I'm **sometimes** late for class.	
never	My parents **never** drink coffee.	0%

Look! *never* has a negative meaning, but we use a positive form.
My children never get up early. **NOT** *My children don't never get up early.*

4C Present simple: *wh-* questions

We ask questions with question words to ask for specific information.

A day / time of day – *When does your brother go to the gym?*
A time – *What time does the class start?*
A thing – *What do you drink at work?*
A person – *Who do you work with?*
A place – *Where do you live?*
A reason – *Why do you get up early on Saturday?*
A number – *How many keys do you have?*
An age – *How old is Julian?*
A manner – *How do you get to work?*

The word order in questions with most verbs is question word + *do/does* + subject + main verb + rest of question.

▶ 4.8	Question word	*do/does*	Subject	Main verb	Rest of question
	What	do	you	have	for breakfast?
	When	does	she	see	her friends?
	Where	do	his parents	work?	

With the verb *be*, the word order in questions is question word + *am/is/are* + subject + rest of question.

▶ 4.9	Question word	am/is/are	Subject	Rest of question
	Why	am	I	cold?
	What time	is	the bus?	
	How	are	you	today?

1 Order the words to make sentences.

1 brother / never / my / up / gets / early
_____.
2 office / I / have / usually / lunch / at / the
_____.
3 trains / late / always / the / night / at / are
_____.
4 always / the / morning / a / have / I / in / shower
_____.
5 dressed / I / get / usually / breakfast / before
_____.
6 friendly / very / is / teacher / my / always
_____.
7 never / we / dinner / before / have / 9.00 p.m.
_____.
8 videos / watch / sometimes / in / we / class
_____.

◀ Go back to page 33

1 Complete the questions with the question words in the box.

How many	What	What time
When	Where	Why

1 _____ does your brother do?
He's a taxi driver.
2 _____ do you usually play tennis?
I usually play at the weekend.
3 _____ does your sister work?
She works at the hospital.
4 _____ do you like your job?
Because I meet a lot of people and it's interesting.
5 _____ does your English class start?
At 7.30 p.m.
6 _____ cousins do you have?
I have eight cousins.

2 Write questions.

1 What / you / want for dinner?
_____
2 Why / he / cycle to work?
_____
3 Who / be / your favourite actors?
_____
4 How / they / know that man?
_____
5 Where / your mum / go shopping?
_____
6 What time / the lesson / finish?
_____

◀ Go back to page 37

5A *can* and *can't*

We use *can* and *can't* (*cannot*) to talk about ability.

I can play the piano.   My grandmother can't drive.

To make questions with *can*, we put *can* before the subject.

Can you speak Portuguese?   What can he cook?

We use the same form for all people and things.

I/You/He/She/It/We/They can swim.

▶ 5.3	I / you / he / she / it / we / they
+	I **can speak** Italian.
–	You **can't play** the violin.
?	**Can** he **cook** Chinese food?
Y/N	Yes, he **can**. / No, he **can't**.

Look! We use *can/can't* with *well* to say we are good/bad at something.
She can speak English well.
They can't swim well.

1 Write positive (+) or negative (–) sentences with *can*.

1 My sister / drive. (–)

_____

2 Dogs / swim. (+)

_____

3 Her son / use a computer. (–)

_____

4 My dad / cook well. (+)

_____

2 Complete the questions. Use *can* and the verbs in brackets. Then write the short answers.

1 A _____ Sarah _____ 10 km? (run)
  B Yes, _____ .
2 A _____ you and Jo _____ salsa? (dance)
  B No, _____ .
3 A _____ your son _____ Italian food? (cook)
  B Yes, _____ .
4 A _____ you _____ well? (sing)
  B No, _____ .

◀ Go back to page 43

5C Object pronouns

The object of a sentence is the noun which comes after the verb.

I like biscuits. (*biscuits* are the object of the sentence)
Ana calls her sister every week. (*her sister* is the object of the sentence)

We use object pronouns instead of nouns when we know what the noun is.

Emily is a really nice person. I like her. (*her = Emily*)
Fruit juice is good for you. I drink it for breakfast. (*it = fruit juice*)

▶ 5.14	Subject pronouns	Object pronouns	
	I	me	I'm here. Can you see **me**?
	you	you	You're friendly. I like **you**.
	he	him	Paul's a doctor. We work with **him**.
	she	her	Who is Karen? I don't know **her**.
	it	it	I love walking. Do you like **it**?
	we	us	We're at work. Call **us** if you have a problem.
	you	you	You and Ben are only 12 years old. Your parents look after **you**.
	they	them	I have three cats. I love **them**!

Look! We always use object pronouns, not subject pronouns, after prepositions.
Can you come with me?
Where's Paul? I want to talk to him.

1 Replace the underlined words with object pronouns.

1 I love <u>books</u>. _____
2 My sister has <u>the car</u>. _____
3 He doesn't like <u>Maria</u>. _____
4 They cook for <u>my wife and me</u>. _____
5 Give the book to <u>John</u>. _____
6 Can he help <u>you and Abdul</u>? _____

2 Choose the correct words to complete the sentences.

1 Ivan's a waiter. I see *he / him* at work.
2 Lucy lives in France, but *she / her* isn't French.
3 I hate cleaning. Why do I do *me / it*?
4 Your children are quiet. Where are *they / them*?
5 This bike is very fast. Do you want *it / them*?
6 Can you look after my plant? *It / Her* needs water every day.

◀ Go back to page 47

Hello Classroom language

1 ▶ 1.7 Listen and repeat.

1 Open your books.

2 Close your books.

3 Go to page 5.

4 Look at the picture.

5 Listen and repeat.

6 Work in pairs.

7 Excuse me, what does 'nice' mean?

8 Sorry, I don't understand.

9 How do you say 'bom dia' in English?

10 Can you repeat that, please?

11 How do you spell that?

12 Sorry I'm late.

2 Complete the conversation with the words in the box.

> go open listen ~~late~~ look spell work close mean repeat

Norio Hello. Sorry I'm ¹___late___ .
Teacher Hello. Are you Norio?
Norio Yes, I am.
Teacher I'm your teacher. My name's Helen.
Norio Hi.
Teacher ²_____ your book and go to page 6, please.
Norio Sorry, can you ³_____ that?
Teacher Yes. ⁴_____ to page 6 in your book.
Norio OK.
Teacher ⁵_____ at the picture of a family.

Norio Excuse me, what does 'family' ⁶_____ ?
Teacher Your mother, father, brothers, sisters ...
Norio I understand. How do you ⁷_____ 'family'?
Teacher F-A-M-I-L-Y.
Norio Thank you.
Teacher ⁸_____ and repeat – 'family'.
Norio Family.
Teacher Very good. Now, ⁹_____ your books and ¹⁰_____ in pairs ...

◀ Go back to page 5

1A Countries and nationalities

1 ▶ 1.12 Listen and repeat.

1 Argentina
Argentinian

2 Brazil
Brazilian

3 Canada
Canadian

4 Chile
Chilean

5 China
Chinese

6 France
French

7 Germany
German

8 India
Indian

9 Italy
Italian

10 Japan
Japanese

11 Mexico
Mexican

12 Peru
Peruvian

13 Poland
Polish

14 Russia
Russian

15 Spain
Spanish

16 Turkey
Turkish

17 the UK
British

18 the USA
American

2 Look at the pictures. Complete the sentences with the correct country or nationality.

1 Lionel Messi is _____ .

2 Paris is in _____ .

3 A kimono comes from _____ .

4 Pasta is _____ food.

5 A panda is an animal from _____ .

6 Washington D.C. is the capital of _____ .

7 Machu Picchu is in _____ .

8 These are _____ dolls.

9 The Taj Mahal is in _____ .

10 Warsaw is a _____ city.

◀ Go back to page 6

1B Jobs

1 ▶ **1.19** Listen and repeat.

1 an actor

2 a chef

3 a doctor

4 an engineer

5 an IT worker

6 an office worker

7 a police officer

8 a receptionist

9 a shop assistant

10 a singer

11 a student

12 a taxi driver

13 a teacher

14 a tour guide

15 a TV presenter

16 a waiter/a waitress

> **Look!** We use *an* with jobs that begin with vowels (*a, e, i, o, u*) and *a* with jobs that begin with consonants (*b, c, d, f,* etc.).
> *I'm **a** teacher.*
> *Are you **an** office worker?*

2 Match the jobs in the box with objects 1–8. Use *a* or *an*.

| waiter   shop assistant   engineer   singer   receptionist   doctor   chef   actor |

1 _____

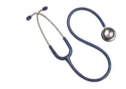
2 _____

3 _____

4 _____

5 _____

6 _____

7 _____

8 _____

◀ Go back to page 8

1C Adjectives (1)

1 ▶ **1.32** Listen and repeat.

1 good 2 bad

3 beautiful 4 ugly

5 big 6 small

7 cheap 8 expensive

9 interesting 10 boring

11 new 12 old

13 happy 14 sad

15 easy 16 difficult

17 old 18 young

2 Choose the correct words to complete the conversations.

A This phone is ¹*cheap / boring*.
It's only £50.
B Yes, but it isn't ²*difficult / good*.
Look at this phone.
A It's £695! It's very ³*expensive / new*.

A How ⁶*good / old* is Michael?
B He's ⁷*new / young*. He's three years old today!
A He's very ⁸*happy / sad*.

A Hi, Sara. Do you understand Italian?
B Yes. I'm Spanish, but Italian is ⁴*big / easy* for me.
A Oh, that's ⁵*interesting / ugly*.

A Wow – this painting is ⁹*beautiful / difficult*!
B Yes, but it's very ¹⁰*bad / small*.
A My house is small, too!

◀ Go back to page 11

2A Personal objects

1 ▶ 2.2 Listen and repeat.

1 a bag

2 a book

3 a camera

4 a credit card

5 glasses

6 keys

7 a mobile phone

8 a pen

9 a pencil

10 a purse

11 sunglasses

12 a tablet

13 an umbrella

14 a wallet

15 a watch

2 Write the objects you can see in the pictures.

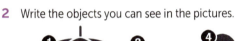

1 _____   4 _____
2 _____   5 _____
3 _____   6 _____

◀ Go back to page 14

2B Colours

1 ▶ 2.8 Listen and repeat.

1 black

2 blue

3 brown

4 gold

5 green

6 grey

7 orange

8 pink

9 purple

10 red

11 silver

12 white

13 yellow

2 Write the colours.

1 red + blue = _____
2 red + white = _____
3 blue + yellow = _____
4 black + white = _____
5 red + yellow = _____
6 red + blue + yellow = _____

◀ Go back to page 16

1C Numbers 0–100

1 ▶ 1.26 Listen and repeat.

0 zero/oh	5 five	10 ten	15 fifteen	20 twenty	50 fifty	100 a hundred/
1 one	6 six	11 eleven	16 sixteen	21 twenty-one	60 sixty	one hundred
2 two	7 seven	12 twelve	17 seventeen	22 twenty-two	70 seventy	
3 three	8 eight	13 thirteen	18 eighteen	30 thirty	80 eighty	
4 four	9 nine	14 fourteen	19 nineteen	40 forty	90 ninety	

2 Write the numbers as words or digits.

1 34 _____   3 63 _____   5 88 _____   7 29 _____   9 12 _____

2 ____ seventy-two   4 ____ ninety-one   6 ____ fifty-seven   8 ____ forty-four   10 ____ a hundred

◀ Go back to page 10

2C Family and friends

1 ▶ 2.10 Listen and repeat.

1 grandfather   2 grandmother

3 grandparents

4 mother   5 father   7 son   8 daughter

6 parents   9 children

10 husband   11 wife   12 sister   13 brother   14 boyfriend   15 girlfriend

2 Look at the family tree. Read the sentences and write the names.

1 My brother is Liam. _____
2 Julia is my wife. _____
3 My sister is Julia and my brother is George. _____
4 My girlfriend is Molly. _____
5 My parents are George and Gloria, and my sister is Molly. _____
6 Bob is my father, and Mark and George are my brothers. _____
7 My wife is Judith. _____
8 My husband's brother is Mark. _____
9 Our children are Julia, Mark and George. _____ and _____
10 Our parents are Judith and Bob. _____ , _____ and _____

Judith   Bob

Tony   Julia   Mark   George   Gloria

Ben   Molly   Liam   Lucy

◀ Go back to page 18

3A Food and drink

1 ▶ 3.2 Listen and repeat.

Food

1 biscuits

2 bread

3 cake

4 cheese

5 chicken

6 chips

7 chocolate

8 crisps

9 eggs

10 fish

11 fruit

12 ice cream

13 meat

14 pasta

15 pizza

16 potatoes

17 rice

18 salad

19 sandwich

20 vegetables

Drinks

21 coffee

22 milk

23 orange juice

24 tea

25 water

Look! If we want to talk about the food and drink that we eat and drink at breakfast, lunch and dinner, we can use the verb *have*.

*What do you **have** for breakfast/lunch/dinner?*
*I **have** coffee for breakfast. I **have** a sandwich for lunch. I **have** fish for dinner.*

08.00

have breakfast

13.00

have lunch

18.30

have dinner

---

2 Choose the correct words to complete the sentences.

1 Ice cream has *milk / cheese* in it.
2 Potatoes are *fruit / vegetables*.
3 Cake, biscuits and *chocolate / salad* are bad for you.
4 Crisps and chips come from *potatoes / pasta*.
5 British people have *rice / milk* in their tea.

6 Spaghetti is a type of *bread / pasta*.
7 I have *breakfast / lunch* at 8.00 a.m.
8 Vegetarians don't eat *meat / salad*.
9 I drink *orange juice / fish* in the morning.
10 I have *chocolate / meat* and vegetables for dinner.

◀ Go back to page 24

3C Common verbs (1)

1 ▶ **3.12** Listen and repeat.

1 change money

2 do exercise

3 go to school

4 have two children

5 know the answer

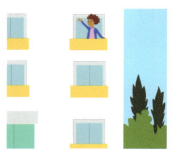

6 live in a flat

7 make coffee

8 say 'goodbye'

9 study German

10 think (about ...)

11 use a tablet

12 want a drink

13 watch a film

14 work in an office

> **Look!** We use *make* for food and drink:
> *They make very good cakes.*
>
> We use *do* for activities:
> *We do exercise in the morning.*
>
> We use *think* for thoughts and opinions:
> *I think about work. (thought)*
> *We think it's a good idea. (opinion)*

2 Choose the correct words to complete the sentences.

1 After work, I *know / go / use* to the gym.
2 I *study / say / live* English and Spanish at university.
3 My daughter and I *make / do / work* cakes at the weekend.
4 I *think / know / work* in a restaurant – I'm a waitress!
5 **A** Do you like that book?
   B No, I *think / watch / use* it's boring.
6 My boyfriend and I *watch / say / live* TV in the evening.

7 Do you *make / do / go* exercise at the weekend?
8 Do they *use / know / live* in a big house?
9 I *study / live / say* 'good morning' to people at work.
10 My mobile phone is old. I *watch / want / work* a new one.
11 **A** What's the capital of China?
   B I don't *go / use / know*.
12 My children *use / say / make* the internet a lot.

◀ Go back to page 28

4A Daily routine verbs

1 ▶ 4.2 Listen and repeat.

1 get up

2 have a shower

3 get dressed

4 leave home

5 start work

6 go shopping

7 listen to the radio

8 do housework / homework

9 finish work

10 get home

11 go to bed

12 read a book

2 Complete the text with the correct form of the verbs in the box.

> do (x2)   get (x3)   go (x2)   leave   finish   listen   start   have

I'm Miranda and this is my typical day. I ¹_____ up at 7.00 in the morning and ²_____ a shower. Then I have breakfast with my son, Leon. He ³_____ dressed and then we ⁴_____ home at about 8.30 a.m. Leon goes to school and I'm an office worker. I ⁵_____ work at 9.00 a.m.
I ⁶_____ work at 3.00 p.m. and go to Leon's school. We ⁷_____ shopping and ⁸_____ home at about 4.00 in the afternoon. In the evening, Leon ⁹_____ his homework and I make dinner. After dinner, Leon ¹⁰_____ to bed at 8.00 p.m. and I ¹¹_____ the housework and ¹²_____ to the radio. I go to bed at 11.00 p.m. … and the next day, we do it all again!

◀ Go back to page 32

4B Transport

1 ▶ 4.6 Listen and repeat.

1 by bike

2 by boat

3 by bus

4 by car

5 by ferry

6 by lorry

7 by motorbike

8 by plane

9 by taxi

10 by train

11 on foot

12 on the subway/underground/metro

Look! Different cities have different names for their underground trains.
*In New York, I go on the **subway**.   In London, I go on the **underground**.   In Sydney, I go on the **metro**.*

2 Match the types of transport in the box with the pictures.

lorry   taxi   underground   ferry   train   plane   boat   motorbike

3 Complete the sentences with the correct types of transport and *by* or *on*.

1 I go _____ 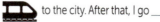 to the train station. Then I go _____ to the city. After that, I go _____ to the office.

2 Lucia goes _____ 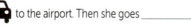 to the airport. Then she goes _____ 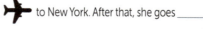 to New York. After that, she goes _____ 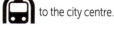 to the city centre.

3 We go _____  to Dover, but my brother goes _____ . Then we all go _____ to France.

◀ Go back to page 34

3B Days and times of day

1 ▶ 3.7 Listen and repeat.

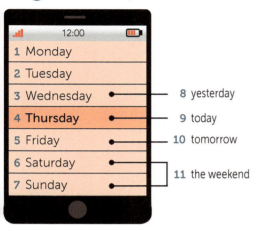

1 Monday
2 Tuesday
3 Wednesday
4 Thursday
5 Friday
6 Saturday
7 Sunday

8 yesterday
9 today
10 tomorrow
11 the weekend

05.00–12.00
12 morning

12.00–18.00
13 afternoon

18.00–21.00
14 evening

21.00–05.00
15 night

Look! We use the preposition *on* with days of the week, *in* with *the morning*, *the afternoon* and *the evening* and *at* with *the weekend* and *night*.

*I eat fish **on** Friday.*
*I have breakfast **in** the morning.*
*I drink milk **at** night.*

We also say *on* + day and time of day:

on Wednesday morning, on Friday afternoon, etc.

2 Chose the correct words to complete the sentences and questions.

1 My birthday is *on / in / at* Sunday.
2 I have dinner *on / in / at* the evening.
3 We don't drink coffee at *afternoon / evening / night*.
4 I have lunch with Emma on *the weekend / Friday / the morning*.
5 Is your English lesson *on / in / at* Thursday evening?
6 They have breakfast at 9.00 in *the weekend / Wednesday / the morning*.
7 Is Marcus on holiday *on / in / at* Thursday?
8 They aren't at university *on / in / at* Wednesday afternoon.
9 What do you have for lunch at *the afternoon / the weekend / Monday*?
10 On Sunday, I have chicken for lunch *on / in / at* the afternoon.

◀ Go back to page 26

4C Adjectives (2)

1 ▶ 4.7 Listen and repeat.

1 cold   2 hot

3 clean   4 dirty

5 fast   6 slow

7 friendly   8 unfriendly

9 nice   10 horrible

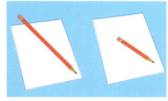

11 large   12 small

13 long   14 short

15 noisy   16 quiet

2 Complete the text with the adjectives in the box.

noisy   cold   quiet   hot   short   friendly   dirty   large

Hi, I'm Matt. I'm a student in Edinburgh, Scotland. I always get up at 8.30 and I have a ¹_____ tea for breakfast. Then I go to the university on foot. It's sometimes ²_____ in the mornings, but that's OK – it's only a ³_____ walk.

I live in a ⁴_____ house with eight students. They're really ⁵_____ . We always make dinner together, and sometimes there are a lot of ⁶_____ dishes when we finish! My housemates play music and the house is sometimes ⁷_____ , so I usually work in the library – it's always ⁸_____ there.

◀ Go back to page 36

5A Common verbs (2)

1 ▶ 5.1 Listen and repeat.

1 arrive at the airport

2 call my mother

3 cook fish

4 dance salsa

5 drive a car

6 give a present

7 help my grandmother

8 look after my daughter

9 meet friends

10 play football

11 play the piano

12 sing

13 speak Italian

14 swim in the sea

15 travel by bus

2 Complete the sentences with the correct form of the verbs in the box.

> cook   meet   give   arrive   help   drive   speak   play (x2)   travel   sing   call   look after

1 Simon _____ Portuguese.
2 I _____ dinner at the weekend.
3 Sharon often _____ basketball.
4 My father _____ a bus.
5 I always _____ my son with his homework.
6 We usually _____ by train.

7 I sometimes _____ my friend's dog.
8 We _____ in Lima at 9.15 a.m.
9 I always _____ Lucy for a coffee after work.
10 You never _____ me flowers.
11 Jo likes music. She _____ and _____ the guitar.
12 My parents live in India, so I _____ them on Skype.

◀ Go back to page 42

5B Electronic devices

1 ▶ 5.8 Listen and repeat.

1 desktop computer

2 DVD player

3 DVR (digital video recorder)

4 earphones

5 headphones

6 laptop

7 MP3 player

8 radio

9 remote control

10 Sat Nav

11 smartphone

12 TV (television)

2 ~~Cross out~~ the word which is incorrect in each sentence.

1 A Listen to this song on my phone – it's great!
  B One moment – I need some *earphones / remote control / headphones*.
2 A Can I check my emails?
  B Yes. You can use my *radio / laptop / smartphone*.
3 A My friend lives on Bridge Street, but I don't know where that is.
  B It's OK. I have *a smartphone / a Sat Nav / an MP3 player*. We can use that.
4 A Do you want to watch a film tonight?
  B We can't, sorry. I don't have a *remote control / TV / DVD player*.

5 A I work at home. I have a *laptop / TV / desktop computer* and that's all I need.
  B At home? What a nice job!
6 A It's quiet. Why don't we listen to some music?
  B OK ... where is the *radio / Sat Nav / MP3 player*?
7 A The news is on at 12.00.
  B OK, the *DVD player / TV / radio* is over there.
8 A Do you have a TV?
  B No, I don't. I watch TV shows on my *laptop / radio / smartphone*.

◀ Go back to page 44

5C Activities

1 ▶ 5.13 Listen and repeat.

1 cleaning

2 cooking

3 cycling

4 dancing

5 going out

6 listening to music

7 meeting friends

8 reading

9 running

10 shopping

11 sleeping

12 swimming

13 walking

14 watching TV/films

Look! We can use activities that end in *-ing* or nouns with the verbs *like*, *love* and *hate*.
I like shopping. I love clothes!
I don't like cycling. I hate bikes.

2 Match the activities in the box with pictures 1–8.

swimming   reading   running   cooking   cycling   cleaning   shopping   sleeping

1 _____

2 _____

3 _____

4 _____

5 _____

6 _____

7 _____

8 _____

◀ Go back to page 46

Hello Student A

1 Look at the labels. Ask Student B for the name of the city.

   A *What's LHR?*
   B *I think it's London.*
   A *How do you spell that?*
   B *L-O-N-D-O-N.*

FINAL DEST.
LHR

1 _____

FINAL DEST.
MEX

2 _____

FINAL DEST.
IST

3 _____

FINAL DEST.
LAX

4 _____

FINAL DEST.
HGK

5 _____

2 Listen to Student B's airport codes. Tell him/her the correct city for the letters.

| New Delhi | Cape Town | Barcelona | New York | Amsterdam |

1A Student A

1 You are Mehmet. Answer Student B's questions with the information.

   B *What's your name?*
   A *I'm Mehmet Guliyev.*
   B *How do you spell that?*
   A *M-E-H-M-E-T …*

Name:	Mehmet Guliyev
Nationality:	Turkish
Phone:	90 312 213 2965

2 Ask Student B the questions and write down his/her answers.

   1 What's your name?
     _____

   2 Where are you from?
     _____

   3 What's your phone number?
     _____

1C Student A

1 Ask Student B questions about the Antarctic Zebras to complete the information.

   Where are they from?   How old is Bev?   What is her job?

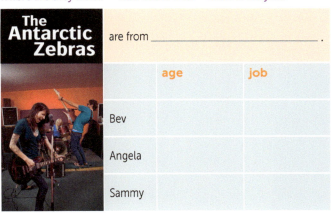

The Antarctic Zebras are from _____ .

	age	job
Bev		
Angela		
Sammy		

2 Now look at the information about the Rocking Stones. Answer Student B's questions.

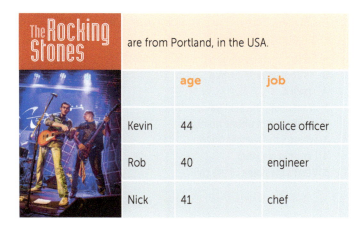

The Rocking Stones are from Portland, in the USA.

	age	job
Kevin	44	police officer
Rob	40	engineer
Nick	41	chef

2A Students A and B

1 Look at the picture. In pairs, ask about the objects.

What's this/that?   What are these/those?

2 Now go to page 143 and check your ideas.

2C Student A

Ask and answer questions with Student B to complete David and Victoria Beckham's family tree.

A *What's David's mother's name?*
B *Her name is ...*

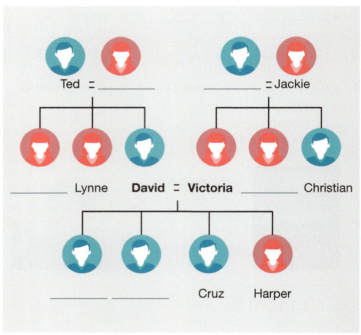

Ted = _____   _____ = Jackie

_____ Lynne   **David** = **Victoria** _____ Christian

Cruz   Harper

_____ _____

2D Student A

1 Ask Student B the questions and write down the answers. Remember to be polite.

A *Excuse me, what time's the next train to Boston, please?*
B *It's at quarter to twelve.*
A *Thanks.*

1 What time's the next train to Boston? _____
2 What's Lucy's phone number? _____
3 Where's the teacher from? _____
4 How old are you? _____
5 What's the name of the café? _____

2 Answer Student B's questions with the answers in the box.

> He's 28.   She's from Mexico.   You're in Room 48.
> It's F-O-S-T-E-R.   It's at 6.40.

3A Student A

1 Ask Student B questions to complete the information.

A *What do you have for breakfast?*
B *For breakfast, I eat ...*

breakfast	lunch	dinner

2 Look at the information. Answer Student B's questions about your breakfast, lunch and dinner.

breakfast	lunch	dinner

3C Student A

1 Ask Student B questions about Magda to complete the information in the table.

A *Does Magda live in a city?*
B *Yes, she does. She lives in Gdansk.*

	Magda	Antonio
work in an office?		✗ (he / work / in a school)
live in a city?		✓
have children?		✓ (he / have / two daughters)
watch TV in the morning?		✗ (he / work)
use public transport every day?		✓
go to the gym after work?		✗ (he / make / dinner)
study in the evening?		✗ (he / watch / TV)
do sport at the weekend?		✓

2 Look at the information about Antonio. Answer Student B's questions and give extra information when you can.

B *Does Antonio work in an office?*   A *No, he doesn't. He works in a school.*

4A Student A

1 Write sentences in the present simple with the adverbs of frequency in brackets. Then read them to Student B.

1 Leila / watch / films on her phone. (sometimes)
_____

2 Dean / wake up / before 6.00 a.m. (often)
_____

3 Paulo / read / in bed. (usually)
_____

4 Marta / be / late for work. (never)
_____

5 Shaun / cook / dinner for his family. (always)
_____

2 Listen to Student B. Match the names in the box with the people.

Danny   Nina   Eric   Claire   Tom

1 _____   2 _____   3 _____   4 _____   5 _____

I usually finish work after 7.00 p.m.

I'm often in the library at night.

I always drink tea for breakfast.

I never have a bath in the morning.

I sometimes go to the gym on Saturday.

4C Student A

1 Ask Student B questions about Ella. Write his/her answers.

A *Where does Ella live?* B *She lives in Manchester.*

Ella	Questions
	Where / live?
	What / do?
	Where / work?
	What time / get up?
	What time / finish work?
	Why / like her job?
	How / relax in the evening?
	What / do at the weekend?

2 Read Zain's profile. Listen to Student B and answer his/her questions.

Zain

Hi, I'm Zain. I live in Los Angeles. I'm a waiter at a big hotel in Hollywood. I get up at 8.00 a.m. and before work I usually go to the gym. I start work at 11.00 and I finish at 9.00 p.m. I like my job because I meet interesting people. To relax in the evening, I play the guitar. I usually work at the weekend.

4D Student A

1 You are a customer. Ask Student B for the things on your shopping list. Then ask how much each thing is. Remember to be polite.

A *Good morning. Can I have a cheese sandwich, please?*
B *Here you are.*
A *Thank you. How much is it?*
B *£1.99. Anything else?*

Shopping list
1 cheese sandwich
6 eggs
some orange juice
some coffee
some pasta
Total price = ?

2 You are a shop assistant. Serve Student B. Remember to be polite.

2x bottles water	$1.60
fish	$5.80
1x pizza (4 cheese)	$3.99
1 box salad	$1.50
1 chocolate cake	$3.85
Total	$16.74

5A Student A

1 Look at the table. Ask questions with *can* to guess which person Student B has.

A *Can she drive?*
B *Yes, she can.*

	Annie	Mona	Sara	Lucy	Hana	Kim
Can / drive?	✗	✓	✓	✓	✓	✓
Can / speak Spanish?	✗	✓	✓	✗	✓	✗
Can / play the guitar?	✓	✗	✓	✗	✓	✗
Can / cook Chinese food?	✓	✓	✗	✓	✗	✗
Can / dance salsa?	✗	✗	✓	✗	✗	✓

2 Answer Student B's questions about Mark. You can only say *Yes, he can* or *No, he can't*.

MARK

He can swim well and write computer programs.
He can't look after children, play the piano or speak French.

5C Student A

1 Look at the profiles for a website called *New Friends*. Ask and answer questions with Student B to complete the information.

A *What does Daniela think about cooking?*   **B** *She likes it.*

☺☺ = love, ☺ = like, ☹ = not like, ☹☹ = hate

Daniela	
	cooking
	cats and dogs
	early mornings

Bill	
	walking
	housework
	books

Monica	
	going out
	cycling
	the cinema

Miguel	
☹	cleaning
☺☺	reading
☹☹	sport

Claudio	
☺	swimming
☺☺	watching films
☹	dancing

Lucy	
☺	sleeping
☺	animals
☺☺	food and drink

2 Look at the profiles again. Find the best new friend for each person.

Hello Student B

1 Listen to Student A's airport codes. Tell him/her the correct city for the letters.

> Hong Kong   Los Angeles   Mexico City   London   Istanbul

A *What's LHR?*
B *I think it's London.*
A *How do you spell that?*
B *L-O-N-D-O-N.*

2 Look at the labels. Ask Student A for the name of the city.

FINAL DEST.
JFK

1 _____

FINAL DEST.
BCN

2 _____

FINAL DEST.
CPT

3 _____

FINAL DEST.
DEL

4 _____

FINAL DEST.
AMS

5 _____

1A Student B

1 Ask Student A the questions and write down his/her answers.

1 What's your name?

_____

2 Where are you from?

_____

3 What's your phone number?

_____

2 You are Saori. Answer Student A's questions with the information.

A *What's your name?*
B *I'm Saori Arakawa.*
A *How do you spell that?*
B *S-A-O-R-I ...*

Name:	Saori Arakawa
Nationality:	Japanese
Phone:	81 90 1790 1357

1C Student B

1 Look at the information about the Antarctic Zebras. Answer Student A's questions.

The Antarctic Zebras	are from Liverpool, in the UK.	
	age	**job**
Bev	19	student
Angela	24	IT worker
Sammy	25	tour guide

2 Now ask Student A questions about the Rocking Stones to complete the information.

Where are they from?   How old is Kevin?   What is his job?

The Rocking Stones	are from _____ .	
	age	**job**
Kevin		
Rob		
Nick		

2A Students A and B

Look at the picture. In pairs, discuss if you were right or wrong.

A *This is a pen.*
B *You're right.*

2C Student B

Ask and answer questions with Student A to complete David and Victoria Beckham's family tree.

B *What's Victoria's mother's name?*
A *Her name is ....*

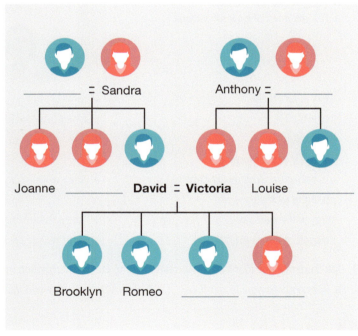

2D Student B

1 Answer Student A's questions with the answers in the box.

> I'm 39.   It's 07700 900638.   The Oak Tree Café.
> It's at 11.45.   He's from Canada.

2 Ask Student A the questions and write down the answers. Remember to be polite.

B *Excuse me, what time's the flight to Los Angeles, please?*
A *It's at twenty to seven.*
B *Thanks.*

1 What time's the flight to Los Angeles? _____
2 How old is the teacher? _____
3 Where's María from? _____
4 What room am I in? _____
5 How do you spell your surname? _____

3A Student B

1 Look at the information. Answer Student A's questions about your breakfast, lunch and dinner.

breakfast   lunch   dinner

2 Ask Student A questions to complete the information.

B *What do you have for breakfast?*
A *For breakfast, I eat …*

breakfast	lunch	dinner

3C Student B

1 Look at the information about Magda. Answer Student A's questions and give extra information when you can.

A *Does Magda live in a city?*
B *Yes, she does. She lives in Gdansk.*

	Magda	Antonio
work in an office?	✓	
live in a city?	✓ (she / live / in Gdansk)	
have children?	✗ (she / have / two cats)	
watch TV in the morning?	✗	
use public transport every day?	✗ (she / walk / to work)	
go to the gym after work?	✓	
study in the evening?	✓ (she / study / English)	
do sport at the weekend?	✗ (she / make / cakes)	

2 Ask Student A questions about Antonio to complete the information in the table.

B *Does Antonio work in an office?*   A *No, he doesn't. He works in a school.*

4A Student B

1 Listen to Student A. Match the names in the box with the people.

| Marta   Shaun   Leila   Dean   Paulo |

1 _____   2 _____   3 _____   4 _____   5 _____

I often wake up before 6.00 a.m.   *I'm never late for work.*   *I usually read in bed.*   *I sometimes watch films on my phone.*   *I always cook dinner for my family.*

2 Make sentences in the present simple with the adverbs of frequency in brackets. Then read them to Student A.

1 Claire / drink / tea for breakfast. (always)

_____

2 Tom / go / to the gym on Saturday. (sometimes)

_____

3 Eric / have / a bath in the morning. (never)

_____

4 Danny / be / in the library at night. (often)

_____

5 Nina / finish / work after 7.00 p.m. (usually)

_____

4C Student B

1 Read Ella's profile. Listen to Student A and answer his/her questions.

A *Where does Ella live?*　　　**B** *She lives in Manchester.*

Ella

Hi, I'm Ella. I live in Manchester. I'm a teacher at a school in the city centre. I usually get up at 6.00 a.m. I start work at 8.30 and I finish at 5.00 p.m. I love my job because I like children. To relax in the evening, I watch TV with my family. At the weekend, I do a lot of sport.

2 Ask Student A questions about Zain. Write his/her answers.

Zain

Questions
Where / live?
What / do?
Where / work?
What time / get up?
What time / finish work?
Why / like his job?
How / relax in the evening?
What / do at the weekend?

4D Student B

1 You are a shop assistant. Serve Student A. Remember to be polite.

A *Good morning. Can I have a cheese sandwich, please?*
B *Here you are.*
A *Thank you. How much is it?*
B *£1.99. Anything else?*

1 sandwich (cheese)	£1.99
6 eggs	£2.50
orange juice	£1.80
coffee	£3.29
pasta	£1.50
Total	£11.08

2 You are a customer. Ask Student A for the things on your shopping list. Then ask how much each thing is. Remember to be polite.

Shopping list
2 bottles of water
some fish
1 four-cheese pizza
1 box of salad
1 chocolate cake
Total price = ?

5A Student B

1 Answer Student A's questions about Hana. You can only say *Yes, she can* or *No, she can't.*

A *Can she drive?*
B *Yes, she can.*

HANA

She can drive, speak Spanish and play the guitar.
She can't cook Chinese food or dance salsa.

2 Look at the table. Ask questions with *can* to guess which person Student A has.

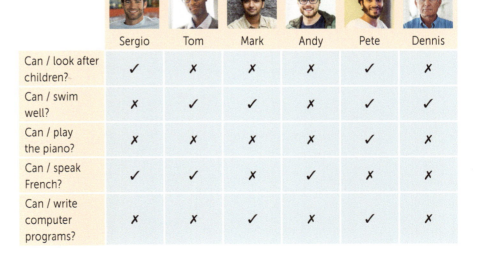

	Sergio	Tom	Mark	Andy	Pete	Dennis
Can / look after children?	✓	✗	✗	✗	✓	✗
Can / swim well?	✗	✓	✓	✗	✓	✓
Can / play the piano?	✗	✗	✗	✗	✓	✗
Can / speak French?	✓	✓	✗	✓	✗	✗
Can / write computer programs?	✗	✗	✓	✗	✓	✗

5C Student B

1 Look at the profiles for a website called *New Friends*. Ask and answer questions with Student A to complete the information.

B *What does Miguel think about cleaning?*   **A** *He doesn't like it.*

☺☺ = love, ☺ = like, ☹ = not like, ☹☹ = hate

Daniela	
☺	cooking
☺☺	cats and dogs
☹	early mornings

Bill	
☹	walking
☹☹	housework
☺	books

Monica	
☹	going out
☹	cycling
☺	the cinema

Miguel	
	cleaning
	reading
	sport

Claudio	
	swimming
	watching films
	dancing

Lucy	
	sleeping
	animals
	food and drink

2 Look at the profiles again. Find the best new friend for each person.

Irregular verbs

Infinitive	Past simple	Infinitive	Past simple
be	was, were	leave	left
become	became	lose	lost
begin	began	make	made
break	broke	meet	met
bring	brought	pay	paid
buy	bought	put	put
choose	chose	read (/riːd/)	read (/red/)
come	came	ride	rode
cost	cost	run	ran
do	did	say	said
drink	drank	see	saw
drive	drove	sell	sold
eat	ate	sit	sat
fall	fell	sleep	slept
feel	felt	spend	spent
find	found	speak	spoke
fly	flew	stand	stood
get	got	swim	swam
give	gave	take	took
go	went	teach	taught
have	had	tell	told
hear	heard	think	thought
hold	held	understand	understood
hurt	hurt	wake	woke
keep	kept	wear	wore
know	knew	win	won
learn	learnt/learned	write	wrote

Personal Best

Workbook

A1
Beginner

My life

GRAMMAR: The verb *be* (*I, you*)

1 Match 1–7 with a–g.

1 ____ you a student?   a Yes
2 Yes, I ____.   b not
3 No, I'm ____.   c I'm a
4 ____, you are.   d Are
5 No, you ____.   e aren't
6 ____ student.   f You're
7 ____ a teacher.   g am

2 (▶) 1.1 Complete the sentences. Listen and check.

A Good morning. ¹_____ you a student?

B Oh, hello. Yes, I ²_____ .

A Welcome to the school. My name's Juan. And you ³_____ … ?

B ⁴_____ Veronika. Nice to meet you. ⁵_____ I in your class?

A No, you ⁶_____ . I'm ⁷_____ your teacher. ⁸_____ in Marek's class.

B OK, thank you.

VOCABULARY: Classroom language

3 Match sentences 1–6 with pictures a–f.

1 Excuse me, what does '*columns*' mean? ____
2 Sorry, I don't understand.   ____
3 How do you say '*arigatou*' in English? ____
4 Can you repeat that, please?   ____
5 How do you spell that?   ____
6 Sorry I'm late.   ____

4 Order the words to make sentences.

1 8 / at / books / page / open / your
   _____ .

2 books / close / your
   _____ .

3 go / 7 / page / to
   _____ .

4 at / look / picture / the
   _____ .

5 and / listen / repeat
   _____ .

6 in / pairs / work
   _____ .

PRONUNCIATION: The alphabet

5 (▶) 1.2 Write the other letters of the alphabet. Listen and check.

1	/eɪ/	n**a**me	Aa, Hh, ____, ____
2	/iː/	s**ee**	Bb, Cc, ____, ____, ____, ____, ____, ____
3	/e/	h**e**llo	Ff, ____, ____, ____, ____, ____, ____
4	/aɪ/	**I**'m	____, ____
5	/əʊ/	n**o**	____
6	/uː/	y**ou**	Qq, ____, ____
7	/ɑː/	**are**	____

GRAMMAR: The verb *be* (*he*, *she*, *it*)

1 Choose the correct words to complete the sentences.

1 **A** *Are / Is* that Donnie Yen?
  B Yes, *it / you* is.

2 **A** Where *am / is* he from?
  B *He's / It's* from Hong Kong.

3 **A** *Am / Is* this restaurant good?
  B Yes! *He's / It's* great!

4 **A** She *aren't / isn't* from Britain. Where's she from?
  B *He's / She's* from Chile.

5 **A** Where *is / are* you from?
  B *I'm / It's* from Valletta.

6 **A** *Where's / Where are* Paris?
  B *It's / She's* in France.

7 **A** *Is / Are* that the Turkish flag?
  B No, it *is / isn't*.

8 **A** Spain's flag *am / is* red and yellow.
  B Yes, *I'm / you're* right.

2 ▶ 1.3 Complete the sentences. Listen and check.

1 I _____ from Peru.

2 Where _____ she from?

3 He _____ American, he's Canadian.

4 _____ you Elena?

5 This _____ Junko. She _____ from Japan.

6 I _____ not Russian.

7 You _____ from Russia. _____ you from Poland?

8 I think he _____ from India.

VOCABULARY: Countries and nationalities

3 Complete the chart.

Country	Nationality
1_____	Canadian
China	2_____
France	3_____
4_____	German
5_____	Indian
Italy	6_____
Peru	7_____
Poland	8_____
Russia	9_____
10_____	British
the USA	11_____
Turkey	12_____

4 Complete the sentences with the correct country or nationality.

1 It's the flag of *Turkey*. (country)

2 It's the *Indian* flag. (nationality)

3 It's the _____ flag.

4 It's the flag of _____.

5 It's the _____ flag.

6 It's the _____ flag.

7 It's the flag of _____.

8 It's the _____ flag.

PRONUNCIATION: Word stress

5 ▶ 1.4 Is the stress on the nationality and country the same (S) or different (D)? Listen, check and repeat.

1 Argentina   Argentinian   _S_
2 China   Chinese   _D_
3 Germany   German   ____
4 Italy   Italian   ____
5 Mexico   Mexican   ____
6 Turkey   Turkish   ____
7 Brazil   Brazilian   ____
8 Japan   Japanese   ____

LISTENING: Listening for information about people

1 ▶ 1.5 Listen and complete the sentences with the words in the box.

> addresses   countries   ~~first names~~
> jobs   nationalities   numbers   surnames

1 They are _first names_.
2 They are _____.
3 They are _____.
4 They are _____.
5 They are _____.
6 They are _____.
7 They are _____.

2 ▶ 1.6 Listen to two conversations. Where are the people?

3 ▶ 1.6 Listen again. Complete the forms.

	Student 1	Student 2
First name	1 _____	Yasin
Surname	Aleksandrov	5 _____
Nationality	2 _____	Turkish
Job	3 _____	6 _____
Classroom	4 _____	7 _____
Teacher	Sandrine	8 _____

4 ▶ 1.7 Listen and correct any contractions.

1 A What is his job?   _What's_
  B He is a student.   _He's_

2 A You are not from Argentina,
     are you?   _____
  B I am from Argentina!   _____

3 A It is not in classroom 8. It is in
     classroom 10.   _____
  B Where is that?   _____

4 A What is her nationality?   _____
  B She is from Canada.   _____

5 A You are a good singer!   _____
  B No, I am not.   _____
  A You are!

6 A I am in Shenzhen.   _____
  B Where is Shenzhen?   _____
  A It is in China.   _____

5 Look at the pictures and complete the job titles.

1 a __ __ __ __
2 e __ __ __ __ __ __ __
3 s __ __ __ __ __ __
4 l __   w __ __ __ __ __
5 r __ __ __ __ __ __ __
6 s __ __ __ __   a __ __ __ __
7 s __ __ __ __ __ __
8 t __ __ __ __   g __ __ __ __
9 T __   p __ __ __ __ __ __ __ __
10 w __ __ __ __ __

GRAMMAR: The verb *be* (*we*, *you*, *they*)

1 Match sentences 1–10 with missing verbs a–c.

1 _____ the books expensive?

2 You and Harpinder _____ good friends.

3 Ursula, Frank and the other students _____ in room 24.

4 _____ we in this classroom today?

5 They _____ sad, they are happy.

6 Liu and I _____ students from China.

7 You _____ a teacher. You're a student.

8 _____ you from Mexico?

9 We _____ the same age. He's 18 and I'm 20.

10 All the chefs here _____ Turkish.

    a are

    b aren't

    c Are

2 Look at the examples. Write sentences with pronouns.

1 her name = Marta
It's Marta.

2 Keith and Sally ≠ American
They aren't American.

3 I ≠ a police officer
_____

4 Pedro and Gabriela = from Brazil?
_____

5 you and Aubert = happy?
_____

6 you and I ≠ old.
_____

7 Elena = 25
_____

8 Michael = in Italy?
_____

9 Yuki and Natsuki = from Japan
_____

10 the book = interesting?
_____

VOCABULARY: Numbers 11–100 and adjectives (1)

3 Write the words for the next two numbers in 1–6.

1 twelve, thirteen, fourteen,
_____, _____ (15, 16)

2 twenty-four, twenty-six, twenty-eight,
_____, _____ (30, 32)

3 one hundred, ninety, eighty,
_____, _____ (70, 60)

4 eleven, twenty-two, thirty-three,
_____, _____ (44, 55)

5 sixty-seven, seventy-three, seventy-nine,
_____, _____ (85, 91)

6 ninety-nine, eighty-five, seventy-one,
_____, _____ (57, 43)

4 ▶1.8 Complete the conversations with the correct adjectives. Listen and check.

1 **A** Are the shoes big?
B No, they're very _____.

2 **A** That dog is ugly.
B Yes, it isn't _____.

3 **A** Is he a _____ singer?
B Yes. He isn't bad.

4 **A** You don't look happy.
B No, I'm not. I'm _____.

5 **A** She's a really boring presenter!
B I don't think she's very _____.

6 **A** Is that watch €89? That's expensive!
B Yes, it isn't _____.

7 **A** This exercise is _____.
B No it isn't. It's easy.

8 **A** You're very _____, aren't you, Grandad?
B No, I'm not! I'm young!

PRONUNCIATION: Numbers

5 ▶1.9 Listen and choose the correct numbers.

1 13   30

2 14   40

3 15   50

4 $16 $60

5 17   70

6 18   80

7 £19   £90

8 40   42

9 52km   62km

10 83   93

WRITING: Completing a form

1 Look at the picture and read the email. Then complete the form for Noemí.

Subject: Happy birthday!

From: Jill

To: nrios@standrews.hosp.ca

Date: 18 May 2018

Hi Noemí!

25 today! Congratulations!

I have a present 🎁 for you.
Are you still at: 28, Olive Road,
Vancouver V5K 1T3?

Lots of love,

J x x x

ST ANDREW'S
HOSPITAL

Vancouver

How can I help?

Dr. Noemí Rios

| Home | Membership | Login | Contact |

To join the gym, complete your personal information.

Title	1 *Dr*
First name	2
Surname	3
Address line 1	4
Address line 2	5
City	6
Post code	7
Email address	8
Phone number	9 *604-509-6995*
Nationality	10
Profession	11
Date of birth (DD/MM/YYYY)	12

Send

2 Read the form then correct the capitals in the sentences below.

First name	Porfirio
Surname	Cubillos
Home city	Guadalajara
Nationality	Mexican
Country of residence	France
Married?	Yes
Wife's name	Claudine
Languages	Spanish, French, English

1 my name is porfirio cubillos.

2 i'm from guadalajara in mexico, but i am in france now.

3 my wife claudine is french.

4 at home, we speak spanish and french.

3 Write similar sentences for you. Remember to use capital letters correctly.

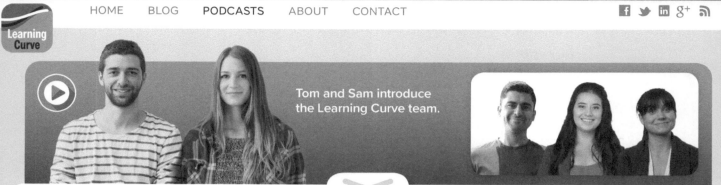

HOME   BLOG   PODCASTS   ABOUT   CONTACT

Tom and Sam introduce
the Learning Curve team.

LISTENING

1 ▶ **1.10** Listen to the podcast about people at Learning Curve. In what order do the people speak? Write 1–5.

a Jack _____

b Penny _____

c Tom _____1_____

d Taylor _____

e Sam _____

2 ▶ **1.10** Listen again. Match the people with the information.

1	Tom _____	a	is a chef.
2	Sam _____	b	is from the USA.
3	Taylor _____	c	is a presenter of Learning Curve.
4	Penny _____	d	works with Tom.
5	Jack _____	e	is British and Argentinian.

3 ▶ **1.10** Listen again. Are the sentences true (T) or false (F)?

1 Every episode of Learning Curve is about food or travel. _____

2 Taylor also presents Learning Curve. _____

3 Taylor is from the USA. _____

4 Penny lives in New York. _____

5 Sam has a restaurant. _____

6 Jack's surname is spelled G-O-O-D-E. _____

READING

1 Read Ethan's blog post about the city of Canberra. Match the people with photos a–c.

1 Chia _____

2 Bill _____

3 Karen _____

2 Read the blog again. Tick (✔) the correct sentences.

1 Canberra is the capital of Australia. _____

2 There are more people in Sydney than in Canberra. _____

3 Canberra is an old city. _____

4 Chia's family are Chinese. _____

5 Chia is a doctor. _____

6 Bill's wife is from Canberra. _____

7 Houses in Canberra are cheap. _____

8 Karen thinks the centre of the city is ugly. _____

9 It is easy to go from Canberra to the countryside. _____

10 Karen doesn't like the weather in Australia. _____

3 Order the letters to make countries or nationalities. Write C or N.

1 A N C H I _____ _____

2 N A P H I S S _____ _____

3 D O L P A N _____ _____

4 C A R N E F _____ _____

5 I N D A N A C A _____ _____

6 U R S A S I _____ _____

7 M A N G E R _____ _____

8 A N P A J _____ _____

9 C E M I X O _____ _____

10 G I A N T A R E N _____ _____

HOME   **BLOG**   PODCASTS   ABOUT   CONTACT

Our guest blogger this week is Ethan. He's in Australia!

COOL CANBERRA!

This week's guest blogger Ethan Moore goes to a fantastic city 'down under'*...

What is the capital city of Australia? Sydney? Melbourne perhaps? No, it's Canberra. Canberra isn't big, like Sydney. And it isn't as old as Melbourne. It's a new city, about a hundred years old. Its population is only 300,000 people. But it's a good city to live in. Three people who live here tell us why Canberra is so good.

Hi. My name's Chia. I love my city! My family is from China but I'm Australian, too. Canberra is small and the people are very friendly. It's great for shopping and it's also very good for jobs. My friends all have good jobs here. They are doctors, receptionists and IT worker. I'm an office worker – I work in a big building in the city centre. But it's only 15 minutes from my house.

Hello. I'm Bill and I'm 24. My wife and I are from Sydney. Sydney is a great city but it's really expensive. A small house costs about $600,000! We can't afford that – I'm a teacher and my wife's a shop assistant. That's why we live in Canberra. It isn't very cheap here but it's less expensive than Sydney. Now we have a small house and we're very happy.

I'm Karen and I'm an engineer – hi! For me, Canberra is the perfect city because it's so beautiful. The city centre is very clean and it's next to a big lake. You are never far from the countryside, and it's easy to get to – just ten minutes away in the car or on your bike! And of course the sky is blue and the weather is perfect for being outside – it's Australia!

* If you go 'down under', you go to Australia or New Zealand.

GRAMMAR: Singular and plural nouns; *this, that, these, those*

1 Write the plural nouns.

1 She's a child. They're _____.
2 It's a country. They're _____.
3 It's a beach. They're _____.
4 He's a person. They're _____.
5 It's a nationality. They're _____.
6 She's a waitress. They're _____.
7 She's a woman. They're _____.
8 It's a box. They're _____.

2 ▶ 2.1 Look at the pictures. Complete the sentences with *this, that, these,* or *those*. Listen and check.

1 _____'s my doctor.

2 _____ is my bag.

3 Are _____ your books?

4 Are _____ his pens?

5 Is _____ a dog?

6 _____ are beautiful dolls!

7 _____ is my house.

8 _____ are very old things.

VOCABULARY: Personal objects

3 Order the letters to make personal objects.

1 His money is in his L A W T E L. _____
2 These S N A G L E S S U S are very expensive. _____
3 You don't have any money? That's OK, you can pay by T R I C E D D R A C. _____
4 I want to buy a small L E T B A T. _____
5 Do you have a M A R E C A to take pictures? _____
6 She keeps her keys in her S U P E R. _____

4 Look at the pictures and complete the sentences.

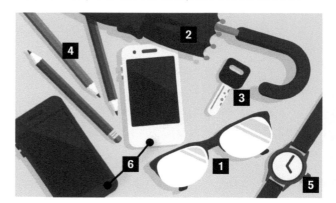

1 They're _____.
2 It's an _____.
3 It's a _____.
4 They're _____.
5 It's a _____.
6 They're _____.

PRONUNCIATION: /ɪ/ and /iː/

5 ▶ 2.2 Which words in 1–10 have the sound /ɪ/? Listen and check.

1 a three b six
2 a listen b repeat
3 a this b these
4 a glasses b mobile phone
5 a he b it
6 a singer b teacher
7 a pen b wallet
8 a cheap b expensive
9 a easy b difficult
10 a keys b credit card

10

READING: Preparing to read

1 Complete the colours.

1 b _ _ _ k, b _ _ e, b _ _ _ n
2 g _ _ _ n, g _ _ y, g _ _ d
3 o _ _ _ _ e
4 p _ _ k, p _ _ _ _ e
5 r _ _
6 s _ _ _ _ r
7 w _ _ _ e
8 y _ _ _ _ w

2 Look at the title and style of the text and the photos. Then choose the correct answers.

1 Where is the text from?
   a a website   c a newspaper
   b a letter

2 What does *prized* mean?
   a expensive   c special
   b old

3 Who wrote the text?
   a one person   b more than one
                              person

3 Read the text. Then read the sentences and write D (Danijela), M (Marko), C (Cheryl) or E (Eugenio).

1 This prized object is beautiful.   _____
2 This person's object goes everywhere
   with them.   _____
3 These are expensive.   _____
4 This object is from a grandparent.   _____
5 His prized object is ugly.   _____
6 His object helps him a lot.   _____
7 Her prized object isn't old.   _____
8 It isn't a small thing.   _____

4 Complete the sentences with the words in the box.

your	very	ugly	prized	photos	old
object	it	is	isn't	his	glasses	family
expensive	earrings	difficult	beautiful	are

1 Danijela says her _____ _____ _____ .

2 Marko can't live without _____ _____ _____ .

3 Cheryl loves her album full of _____ _____ _____ .

4 Eugenio loves the painting, but _____ _____ _____ .

5 And you? What is _____ _____ _____ ?

6 This exercise _____ _____ _____ _____ .
   It's easy!

Our most prized objects

We all have objects we love for different reasons. Here are some people with their prized objects. And you? What's your special object?

Danijela, Slovenia

The important things in my life aren't objects, they're my friends and family. But I have a beautiful pair of earrings from my grandmother. They aren't expensive but I don't want to lose them.

Marko, Russia

I can't live without my glasses – they are my window to the world! Sometimes I can't find them and it's difficult without them. They're a very expensive Italian pair. I've had these glasses for years, but they're still fantastic.

Cheryl, Philippines

My photo album is my most prized object. There are lots of family photos in it from when we were children. Some are twenty years old (they were my mother's), but I collected the photos in a new album last year. I take it with me everywhere.

Eugenio, Costa Rica

I love this painting of my great grandfather (my grandfather's father). It's special because my father gave it to me. But my wife doesn't like it, and it's very big, so we don't have it in the house. It is a bit ugly, but I like it!

11

GRAMMAR: Possessive adjectives; 's for possession

1 Choose the correct words to complete the sentences.

1 Hi, *your / our / my* name's Nadya. Nice to meet you.

2 Rio de Janeiro is famous for *my / its / his* beaches.

3 That's Bozhi. He's a police officer. And that's *her / his / their* girlfriend with him.

4 We live in Sofia, but *our / your / its* home city is Varna.

5 And you? What's *my / her / your* name?

6 My parents live near the sea. You can see it from *his / its / their* house.

7 What about you and your boyfriend? What are *your / his / my* jobs?

8 What's *our / your / her* job? Is she a doctor?

9 I'm a student. *Our / Their / My* classmates are great!

10 These are my dogs and that's *his / its / their* bed.

2 Complete the sentences. Use 's for possession.

1 He's the teacher. Those are his books.
Those are <u>the teacher's</u> books.

2 This is my mother. That's her umbrella.
That's my _____ umbrella.

3 She's Anna. That's her room.
That's _____ room.

4 He's the tour guide. This is his camera.
This is the _____ camera.

5 That's Hugo. This is his laptop.
It's _____ laptop.

6 She's the engineer. Those are her keys.
Those are the _____ keys.

7 That's my friend. This is his wallet.
This is my _____ wallet.

8 He's the chef. That's his hat.
That's the _____ hat.

VOCABULARY: Family and friends

3 Read the text and choose the correct options to complete the sentences.

Hi! I'm Tuyen. This is my family. Hung is my [1] *daughter / husband / sister*, and we have two [2] *children / daughters / sons*. Their names are Nhung and Vien. Nhung is six and her little [3] *brother / sister / son* is three. Vien has the same name as his [4] *grandmother / grandfather / husband*, my father, but we live with my husband's [5] *grandchildren / parents / wives*. Hung's [6] *father's / son's / husband's* name is Tuan and Tuan's [7] *daughter / sister / wife* is called Thu. They're wonderful, and it's great for the children to live with their [8] *grandfathers / grandparents / girlfriends*.

Kim, my husband's [9] *mother / sister / wife*, also lives with us. She's the photographer! She isn't married but she has a [10] *boyfriend / wife / husband*. His name's Chi.

4 Complete the sentences with the correct words.

1 Thu is Hung and Kim's _____.

2 Kim is Chi's _____.

3 Kim is Tuan and Thu's _____.

4 Thu is Nhung and Vien's _____.

5 Hung is Kim's _____.

6 Tuyen is Hung's _____.

7 Vien is Hung and Tuyen's _____.

8 Hung and Tuyen are Nhung and Vien's _____.

PRONUNCIATION: 's

5 ⏵2.3 Say the sentences. Pay attention to the 's sound. Then listen, check and repeat.

1 Is that Giorgio's mother?

2 They're Karina's sunglasses.

3 That watch is Evgeny's.

4 She's Pierre's sister.

5 Alexi's mobile phone is silver.

6 That's the doctor's son.

SPEAKING: Telling the time

1 ▶ 2.4 Listen to the three conversations. Then choose the correct options to complete the sentences.

1 The time now is
  a ten past nine.
  b half past nine.
  c twenty past nine.

2 The film starts at
  a five past eight.
  b quarter to eight.
  c eight o'clock.

3 The meeting usually finishes at
  a half past seven.
  b half past nine.
  c ten o'clock.

2 ▶ 2.4 Listen again. What polite words do you hear? Tick (✔) the words that you hear.

	Conversation		
	1	2	3
Excuse me	✔		
Please			
Sorry			
Thanks			
Thank you			

3 In which conversation in exercise 1 and 2 is the person not polite?

4 Read the answers and write the questions.

1 A What time/in Tokyo?
_____
  B It's three a.m. there now.

2 A What time/train/to Birmingham?
_____
  B It's in half an hour, at ten past eleven.

3 A time/your flight?
_____
  B It's at half past six.

4 A What time/now?
_____
  B It's quarter to three.

5 A Excuse me, what/time?
_____
  B Sorry, I don't know. I don't have a watch.

6 A What time/the lesson?
_____
  B It's at five o'clock, in twenty minutes.

5 Order the words to make sentences. Then match them with questions a–d.

1 forty-five / four / is / it / p.m. / there
_____

2 about / in / minutes / one / ten / there's
_____

3 almost / is / it / o'clock / twelve
_____

4 a.m. / at / it / on / opens / Saturdays / ten
_____

  a What time is the shop open? ____
  b What's the time? ____
  c What time is it in Cairo? ____
  d What time's the next bus into town? ____

HOME   BLOG   PODCASTS   ABOUT   CONTACT

Learning Curve

Tom and Sam talk about an online shop.

LISTENING

1 ▶ 2.5 Listen to the podcast about an online shop called 'yourfavouritethings.com'. Tick (✔) the things you hear.

a   watch   _____
b   camera   _____
c   tablet   _____
d   sunglasses   _____
e   pencils   _____
f   keys   _____
g   pen   _____
h   umbrella   _____
i   credit card _____
j   bag   _____

2 ▶ 2.5 Listen again. Write T (true) or F (false).

1 Sam likes Tom's new watch.   _____
2 Tom's watch is cheap.   _____
3 Abbey's customers answer a lot of questions.   _____
4 Abbey gives Tom a small box.   _____
5 Tom lives in London.   _____
6 Tom goes to the gym.   _____
7 Tom is never late.   _____
8 Abbey's customers only pay for the things they like. _____
9 Tom likes Abbey's idea.   _____
10 The umbrella in the box costs $50.   _____

READING

1 Read Kate's blog about families. Choose the best summary for each person.

Selma

a   Selma is unhappy because her parents are tired and poor.
b   Selma is happy because she is going to university soon.
c   Selma's family is not perfect but she is happy.

Nicolás

a   Nicolás is sad because his family has a small house and a small car.
b   Nicolás likes being an only child because it's quiet and his family has money.
c   Nicolás is happy because his parents are always out in the evenings.

2 Choose the correct options to complete the sentences.

1 Kate's parents have *two / three / four* children.
2 Selma's parents spend a lot of money on *games / food / clothes*.
3 Selma goes out with her *brothers / parents / sisters*.
4 Selma is sad about leaving her *brothers and sisters / parents / country*.
5 Nicolás thinks his parents have a(n) *easy / difficult / boring* life.
6 Nicolás's parents spend a lot of money on *taxis / presents / sport*.
7 Nicolás goes out with his *parents / grandparents / cousins*.

HOME   **BLOG**   PODCASTS   ABOUT   CONTACT

Our guest blogger this week is Kate.

BIG family or small family?

Are you from a big family or a small family? My family isn't big and it isn't small. I only have one brother and no sisters. But some families have a lot of children, and other families only have one child. But which are better – big families with all the fun and noise or small families with peace and quiet? Let's hear from two people with very different families, Selma and Nuria.

Selma: I have two brothers and three sisters and we all live with our parents. I'm eighteen years old and the others are seventeen, fourteen, eleven, seven and two. I think my mother and father are very tired! Having two sons and four daughters is expensive for our parents and they never have any money. I think it's because my brothers eat so much! Our parents only own one expensive thing – a very big car! But I think big families are great for the children. My brothers and sisters are my friends and we are like a team. We argue and fight sometimes, but at the end of the day we are a family. My sisters and I go out together and my younger brothers and sisters always play together. And with so many brothers and sisters, life is never boring! I start university in Germany next year and I'm sad about leaving them.

Nicolás: I am an only child and it's nice. I think my parents are happy, too! We live in a small house and our car isn't big but that means we have more money to spend on other things. Every year we fly to Argentina to see my grandmother and my parents have money to enjoy their life. My father plays golf every weekend and my mother goes to classes with her friends in the evening. Their lives aren't difficult! They buy me a lot of expensive presents, too! And I never need a taxi to get home from parties because my father drives me everywhere! Sometimes I wish I had brothers and sisters to talk to. But I'm not alone – I have my girlfriend, my cousins and my friends to go out with. And everything is calm and quiet in my family. Big families are so noisy!

Food and drink

3A LANGUAGE

GRAMMAR: Present simple (*I*, *you*, *we*, *they*)

1 Choose the correct words to complete the conversations.

1 A *Do you like / Are you like / You do like* this book?
   B Yes, I *do / eat / like*.

2 A *Are / Be / Do* your friends play tennis?
   B *Do they play / They do play / They play* tennis every Sunday.

3 A Fruit cake? No, thanks. I *don't want / want / do want* it.
   B Oh, really? *Do I love / I do love / I love* fruit cake!

4 A *Am / Do / Is* that food good to eat?
   B No, it isn't. Well, I *am not like / don't like / like* it.

5 A Where *do want you / do you want / you do want* to go?
   B Nowhere, thanks. I *don't have / have / do have* enough time.

6 A *Do you / Are you / You do* know Maria?
   B No, but *do I / I don't / I* know her sister, Bella.

2 Rewrite the sentences. Use positive **(+)**, negative **(–)** or question **(?)** forms.

1 I eat an apple every day.
   (–) *I don't eat an apple every day.*

2 We don't have lessons at eight o'clock.
   (+) _____

3 He is a taxi driver.
   (?) _____

4 Do they watch TV?
   (–) _____

5 They study English every day.
   (?) _____

6 Do you have a credit card?
   (+) _____

7 She is very happy.
   (–) _____

8 You speak Italian.
   (?) _____

VOCABULARY: Food and drink

3 Order the letters to make food and drink words.

1 Brown D A B E R _____ W I N D C H A S E S _____ are good for you.

2 Does he drink O F F E C E _____ black or with L I K M _____?

3 Let's cook something quick like T A P S A _____.

4 I love the Z I P S A Z in Italy. _____.

5 Vegans don't eat T A M E _____ or S G E G _____.

6 Have some E T W A R _____ or A R N G O E C E I J U _____

4 Look at the photos and complete the crossword.

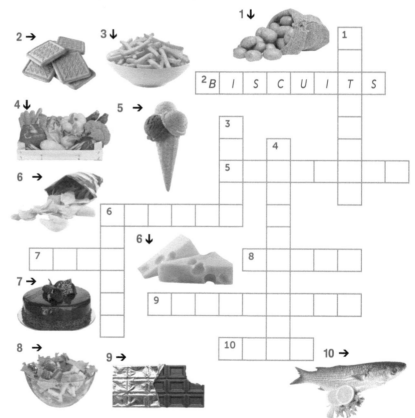

PRONUNCIATION: *do you* /djuː/

5 ▶ 3.1 Listen and complete the questions. Repeat the questions.

1 _____ crisps?
2 _____ cake?
3 _____ Spanish food?
4 _____ milk in China?
5 _____ dinner?
6 _____ for breakfast?

LISTENING: Listening for times and days

1 ⏵ 3.2 Listen to the three conversations. Match the conversations with the places.

1 _____   **a** at a tourist information office
2 _____   **b** at a train station
3 _____   **c** at home
                d in a restaurant
                e in a shop

2 ⏵ 3.2 Listen again. Tick (✔) the days and times you hear.

	Day			Time		
Conversation 1	today	_____	Friday _____	7.15	_____	7.50 _____
Conversation 2	Tuesday	_____	Thursday _____	9.00	_____	19.00 _____
Conversation 3	Monday	_____	Wednesday _____	2.15 p.m.	_____	2.50 p.m. _____

3 ⏵ 3.3 Listen to six conversations and complete the sentences.

1 One orange juice _____ two teas, please.
2 What day's good _____ you?
3 That's _____ twentieth _____ May.
4 There's _____ bus _____ half past three.
5 When _____ you want to meet _____ coffee?
6 Do you have _____ green bag?

4 Complete the calendar with the correct words.

		¹ _y e s t e r d a y_	today	² _ _ _ _ _ _ _		Week Month Year
	³M _ _ _ _ _	⁴T _ _ _ _ _ _	⁵W _ _ _ _ _ _ _ _	⁶T _ _ _ _ _ _ _	⁷F _ _ _ _ _	the ⁸w _ _ _ _ _ _ (Saturday and ⁹S _ _ _ _ _)
6– 12.00	in the morning		8.00 play tennis with Marina			
12– 18.00	in the ¹⁰a _ _ _ _ _ _ _ _		13.30 have lunch - Gustozo's			
18.00– 22.00	in the ¹¹e _ _ _ _ _ _		18.00-21.00 study for exam			
22.00– 00.00	at ¹²n _ _ _ _		22.00 call James			

GRAMMAR: Present simple (*he*, *she*, *it*)

1 Order the words to make sentences. Write the correct capital letters.

1 **A** Ciudad Juarez / does / Gabi / in / live

_____?

B No she doesn't. lives / Monterrey / in / she

_____.

2 **A** does / Lionel / study / where

_____?

B goes / he / the University of London / to

_____.

3 **A** doesn't / have / any money / Naomi

_____.

B does / some today / need / she

_____?

4 **A** doesn't / your / phone / why / work

_____?

B I don't know. anything / do / doesn't / it

_____.

5 **A** at the weekend / does / Halcon / sports / watch

_____?

B Yes. he / likes watching / rugby / tennis and

_____.

2 Complete the sentences with the verbs in the correct form of the present simple.

1 Giovanna _____ (not go) to work until 7 o'clock.

2 Alexia _____ (watch) TV all day on Sundays!

3 _____ (Yannick change) some money before he travels?

4 This watch _____ (not work). It's very old.

5 Evgeny _____ (speak) to his parents every weekend.

6 Ceri is busy on Saturdays. She _____ (study) in the morning.

7 _____ (Vineet do) much exercise?

8 _____ (Nils want) the pasta or a pizza?

9 Her husband _____ (not like) tea or coffee.

10 _____ (you have) a car or a bicycle?

VOCABULARY: Common verbs (1)

3 Match the two parts of the sentences.

1 Do you want   _____
2 I go   _____
3 We live in   _____
4 I don't know the   _____
5 Oliver, say   _____
6 On Friday evenings we watch _____
7 I don't work   _____
8 She studies   _____

a answer. Do you?
b a coffee or a cold drink?
c a house, not a flat.
d to school by train.
e a film, either a DVD or on the internet.
f goodbye to your grandmother.
g Japanese as a hobby.
h in an office.

4 Complete the sentences with the correct verbs.

1 Do you _____ to school or university?

2 He doesn't want to _____ TV all day.

3 Most people _____ a computer these days.

4 My brother and sister _____ lunch for the family at weekends.

5 She doesn't _____ much sport except running.

6 We _____ a black and white cat called 'Pudding'.

PRONUNCIATION: -*s* and -*es* endings

5 ▶ 3.4 Put the verbs in the correct column. Then listen and check.

| changes | ~~eats~~ | goes | knows | lives |
| makes | uses | watches | works | |

/s/	/z/	/ɪz/
eats	_____	_____
_____	_____	_____
_____	_____	_____

WRITING: Punctuation

1 Read the blog and choose the correct photo (a, b or c).

Lucia in Cadiz

| ABOUT | LATEST POST | CONTACT |

Hello! My name's Lucia. This blog is all about my city, Cadiz in Spain.

☆ Carnival! ☆ ☆ ☆ ☆ ☆ ☆ ☆ ☆ ☆

It's February, and every year at this time we celebrate Carnival, a time for singing, eating and friends. There's lots to talk about – the singing competition,

Insert photo here

the fancy dress, the people, etc. – but in this post I want to tell you about the food.

People buy food and eat it in the street. Cadiz is next to the sea and it is famous for its seafood: fish and other things from the sea. In the photo you can see *erizos*. They are ugly but I love them! But my favourite food during Carnival are the sweet biscuits called *pestiños*. They aren't good for you but they're delicious!

2 Rewrite the sentences with the correct punctuation and capital letters.

1 Lucia is from spain.
_____

2 Carnival isnt in February.
_____

3 In Carnival, people like singing eating and seeing their friends
_____

4 people don't usually eat food in restaurants in Carnival.
_____

5 lucia thinks *erizos* are beautiful.
_____

6 Lucia's favourite food isn't good for you?
_____

3 Are the sentences in exercise 2 True or False? Write T or F.

1 ____   3 ____   5 ____
2 ____   4 ____   6 ____

4 Match the two parts of the sentences.

1 She likes ice cream but ____
2 My grandfather is quite old but ____
3 Sandra shops at the supermarket but ____
4 I work in a big office and ____
5 The festival is called New Year but ____
6 Frida has a good job and ____

a he still plays sports.
b we buy vegetables at the market.
c I love it!
d she's very happy.
e it isn't on 1st January.
f her brother prefers fruit.

5 Write a plan for a blog post about a family celebration in your house, e.g. a birthday or holiday. Answer these questions.

- When is the celebration and why do you celebrate it?
- What do you do on the day?
- What special food do you have?
- What's your favourite part of the celebration?

6 Write your blog post. Remember to:

- use correct punctuation and capital letters.
- use the linkers *and* and *but*.

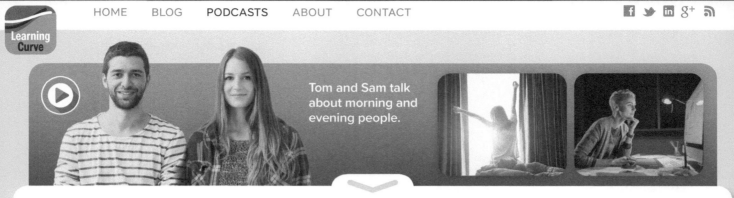

Tom and Sam talk about morning and evening people.

LISTENING

1 ▶ 3.5 Listen to the podcast about 'morning people' and 'evening people'. For each of the people Sam interviews (1–4) write MP (morning person), EP (evening person) or B (both).

1 _____
2 _____
3 _____
4 _____

2 ▶ 3.5 Listen again. Complete each sentence with one word from the podcast.

1 Sam thinks Tom is an _____ person.
2 Sam asked four different people the _____ question yesterday.
3 Speaker 1's job is an _____.
4 Speaker 1 works every _____.
5 Speaker 2 is a _____.
6 Speaker 2's _____ sleep in the morning.
7 Speaker 3 works in a _____.
8 Speaker 3 sometimes sleeps in a quiet _____.
9 Speaker 4 works during the _____.
10 Speaker 4 says _____ are expensive at night.

READING

1 Read Jack's blog about cooking. Match paragraphs 1–4 with photos a–d.

1 _____
2 _____
3 _____
4 _____

2 Read the blog again. Choose the correct answers.

1 The food Jack likes is _____.
  a expensive and difficult to cook
  b expensive and easy to cook
  c cheap and easy to cook
2 Jack says people can _____ for quick recipes.
  a look in a book
  b look on the internet
  c ask a chef
3 Jack says a simple pasta dish can take _____ to cook.
  a ten minutes
  b 30 minutes
  c three hours
4 Jack says chefs _____ learning to cook.
  a don't spend a long time
  b spend a long time
  c don't like
5 Jack says _____ aren't expensive.
  a meat and fish
  b vegetables
  c pasta and tomatoes
6 Jack thinks the best thing people can do is _____.
  a buy food from near where they live
  b buy food from other countries
  c grow their own food
7 Jack says food that _____ can be bad for the planet.
  a is expensive
  b comes from other countries
  c is difficult to cook

HOME　**BLOG**　PODCASTS　ABOUT　CONTACT

Our guest blogger this week is Jack.

KEEP IT simple

Many people think all the best meals are very expensive and difficult to cook. But it just isn't true! Most of my favourite dishes are very easy to make, and cheap, too! Let's look at four ways to make cooking cheap and easy, and why it's important.

1 It's true that many of the most famous dishes in good restaurants take a long time to cook. In fact, sometimes chefs start a meal days before they serve it! But most people don't have three hours to cook a meal every evening. The good news is there are hundreds of quick recipes online – meals that take less than 30 minutes from start to finish. For a very quick meal, a plate of pasta and tomato sauce only takes ten minutes!

2 Chefs study how to cook for years and we can do a lot of different things in the kitchen. But some of my favourite dishes are very, very simple. A piece of fish with some fresh vegetables is delicious, and really easy to cook. Because it only uses a few ingredients, the taste is clean and fresh.

3 In many restaurants you spend a lot of money to have a nice meal. But good food isn't always expensive. In most countries, good meat and fish is expensive but vegetables are cheap. And food from other countries often costs a lot of money. It's better to buy food from your own country. Or even better, grow your own food!

4 Cheap, simple, local food is good for you and it's good for the planet. Food from other countries often travels hundreds of miles by aeroplane. This is bad for everyone. That's another reason to use food from near where you live.

Go to my website for lots of cheap and easy recipes. Or come to my restaurant and let me cook for you!

Daily life

4A | **LANGUAGE**

GRAMMAR: Adverbs of frequency

1 Choose the correct place in each sentence for the adverb in brackets: (a), (b) or (c).

1 I (a) have (b) lunch (c) at 1 o'clock. (*usually*)
2 (a) He (b) drinks hot milk (c). (*never*)
3 Good sunglasses (a) are (b) expensive (c). (*often*)
4 We (a) watch (b) a film on Friday night (c). (*always*)
5 My sister and I (a) are (b) together (c) at the weekends. (*sometimes*)
6 Engineers (a) use (b) a computer (c) all day. (*often*)
7 (a) They (b) leave class (c) early. (*never*)
8 (a) Marco (b) is (c) late for work! (*always*)

2 Look at the calendar. Then complete the sentences about Shruthi's day. Use adverbs of frequency.

Monday	Tuesday	Wednesday	Thursday	Friday
6.30 do sport	**6.30** do sport	**6.30** do sport	**6.45** do sport	**6.30** do sport
7.45 have breakfast with Ana	**7.45** have breakfast with Ana	**7.45** have breakfast with Ana		**7.45** have breakfast with Ana
8.30–6.00 work	**8.30–6.30** work	**8.30–6.00** work	**8.30–6.30** work	**8.30–6.00** work
	1.00 pm go to Carluccio's restaurant		**1.30 pm** go to Brown's restaurant	**1.00 pm** go to El Toro restaurant
6.00 leave work	**6.30** leave work	**6.00** leave work	**6.30** leave work	**6.00** leave work
6.30 pm study Japanese	**7.00 pm** study Japanese		**7.00 pm** study Japanese	
7.30 watch TV	**9.30** watch TV	**8.45** watch TV	**9.00** watch TV	**8.00 pm** see film at the cinema

1 Shruthi ___*always does sport*___ before 7.00 am.
2 She _____ breakfast with Ana.
3 She _____ from half past eight.
4 She _____ to a restaurant for lunch.
5 She _____ work before 6.00 pm.
6 She _____ studies Japanese after work.
7 She _____ a film at the cinema.
8 She _____ TV in the evenings.

VOCABULARY: Daily routine verbs

3 Order the letters to make daily routine verbs.

I'm a chef so I have a long day. I ¹ *teg pu* _____ at seven o'clock and wake my children up. After I ² *teg ddeerss* _____, I make breakfast. Mornings are the only time I see the children. We ³ *aeelv ehmo* _____ at eight thirty – I don't ⁴ *arstt korw* _____ until eleven but I take the children to school before that. My job is difficult and I don't ⁵ *fiihns krow* _____ until eleven o'clock! I always ⁶ *aehv a ehrosw* _____ before I ⁷ *og ot bde* _____ at night.

4 Look at the pictures. Complete the sentences with daily routine verbs.

1 She _____ when she is on the bus.

2 I usually _____ in the mornings.

3 We _____ together in our bedroom.

4 He doesn't _____ early in the evening.

5 They _____ in town every Sunday.

6 Do you _____ when you go to bed?

PRONUNCIATION: Sentence stress

5 ▶ 4.1 Listen to the sentences. Pay attention to the sentence stress. Listen again and repeat.

1 I never have breakfast at a café.
2 He sometimes studies at the weekend.
3 It's often cold here at night.
4 They usually eat salad with lunch.
5 We always watch TV on the computer.
6 She never says 'thank you'.

READING: Finding specific information

1 Complete the sentences with transport words.

1 This is another word for *subway* or *metro*. _____
2 This goes very fast, like a car, but has two wheels. _____
3 This is like a boat and is usually very big. _____
4 You can pay someone to drive you in this car. _____
5 Lots of people pay to go to work by road on this. _____
6 This has two wheels and you can ride it for exercise. _____
7 You can travel by air to other countries in this. _____
8 This doesn't go on the road or under the ground. _____

2 Read the article about five people's journeys. Match each person with the correct transport. You can use more than one letter.

1 Giovanna _____ a bike
2 Jiang _____ b bus
3 Lupita _____ c ferry
4 Gary _____ d on foot
5 Henry _____ e plane
  f the subway

3 Read the article again. Choose the correct options to complete the sentences. Where in the text is the information?

1 The article is about people's *favourite / difficult / daily* journeys.
2 The *vaporetto* is a *plane / bus / train*.
3 Jiang travels for *30 minutes / two and a half hours / five hours* every day.
4 It's difficult for Lupita to *study at home / go to school / get home*.
5 In some parts of Australia, doctors travel by *boat / motorbike / plane*.
6 Henry goes by bike because it is *cheap / clean / fast*.

4 Complete the sentences with a person's name or a place from the article. Then choose P for possession or C for contraction.

1 _____'s Australian.
   P   C
2 Singapore, _____'s city, is perfect for bikes.
   P   C
3 _____'s job is in Venice.
   P   C
4 _____'s a school student.
   P   C
5 Nanjing university is not near to _____'s home.
   P   C
6 Giovanna uses _____'s public transport.
   P   C

It isn't always easy to get to the place you want. Many people study or work far from their homes. Here are five people with interesting daily journeys.

Giovanna is a tour guide in Venice, Italy. Like many people, she travels around by *vaporetto*, the local 'bus' service... except in Venice, these buses don't go on the road, they are ferries! 'I love my journey to work,' she says.

Jiang studies in Nanjing, China. His university is a long way from home. He takes two buses, the subway, then walks for 30 minutes. His total journey time? Two and a half hours each way!

Lupita's house is in the mountains in Colombia but her school is a long way down the mountain. She goes on foot. 'Going to school is easy,' she says, 'but getting home is very difficult!'

Gary is one of Australia's 'flying doctors'. He often goes long distances to see his patients, sometimes hundreds of miles. How? By plane!

Henry gets everywhere really fast in his city, Singapore. 'This is the perfect city to use a bike,' he says. 'It's so safe and easy.'

GRAMMAR: Present simple: *wh-* questions

1 Match questions 1–9 with answers a–i. Then complete the questions with the words in the box.

> how   ~~how many~~   how old   what
> what time   when   where   who   why

1 _How many_ brothers and sisters do you have? _e_
2 _____ do people here do at the weekends? ____
3 _____ is Greta happy? ____
4 _____ does the lesson start? ____
5 _____ is he? ____
6 _____ do your parents live? ____
7 _____ is that girl on the TV? ____
8 _____ do they get to work? ____
9 _____ is her birthday? ____

a At 9.45, I think.
b They go on the underground.
c It's next Tuesday.
d She's a singer.
e ~~I have two sisters.~~
f In a beautiful place called Poole.
g Most people go to the beach.
h He's three today!
i Because she has a new job.

2 Order the words to make questions. Add *do*, *does*, *am*, *is* or *are*.

1 film / what / your favourite
   _____?
2 how / know / the answer / they
   _____?
3 by car / Casey / go / to school / why
   _____?
4 old / your mother / how
   _____?
5 finish / Jerry / time / what / work
   _____?
6 glasses / my / where
   _____?
7 how / you live / many / people / with
   _____?
8 the teacher / this / morning / where
   _____?
9 get / home / when / your / brother
   _____?
10 in the class / know / who / you
   _____?

VOCABULARY: Adjectives (2)

3 ▶ 4.2 Complete the conversations with a pair of words in the box in the correct order. Listen and check.

> clean/dirty   cold/hot   long/short
> horrible/nice   noisy/quiet

1 A Is it _____ in here?
   B No, it's only 13°. I'm quite _____.
2 A You're very _____! I want to listen to the radio.
   B Sorry, Mum. I'll be _____.
3 A I don't want to watch a _____ film. It's late.
   B OK. This film is very _____ – only 80 minutes.
4 A Is your pizza _____?
   B No! It's _____. I really don't like this cheese.
5 A I'm very _____ from doing the housework.
   B Yes, now the house is _____ but you aren't! Have a shower.

4 Complete each sentence with the correct adjective.

1 Buy a s __ __ __ __ cake because not many people know about the party.
2 I love Mexico. It's interesting and the people are very f __ __ __ __ __ __ __.
3 It takes six hours to the city on the s __ __ __ train, but the tickets are cheap.
4 New electric cars are quiet and they are also f __ __ __.
5 Our hotel room is fantastic. It has a really l __ __ __ __ bed.
6 We never go to that supermarket – the shop assistants are so u __ __ __ __ __ __ __ __ __!

PRONUNCIATION: Question words

5 ▶ 4.3 Listen to the questions. Are *do* and *does* stressed? Listen again, check and repeat.

1 When do you listen to the radio?
2 What books does he read?
3 How many films do they watch each week?
4 Who does she go to the cinema with?
5 Why do you like shopping?
6 What time do you study?

SPEAKING: Shopping for food

1 ▶ 4.4 Look at the pictures and listen to a customer in a shop. Does the customer buy a, b or c?

3 ▶ 4.5 Look at the photos and listen to three conversations. Match the conversations (1–3) with the photos (a–c).

1 _____ 2 _____ 3 _____

2 ▶ 4.4 Choose the correct options to complete the conversation. Then listen again and check.

1 How _____ I help you?
   a do   b can   c am

2 Do _____ have fruit juice?
   a you   b I   c we

3 _____ I have orange juice, please?
   a Do   b Am   c Can

4 How _____ is that?
   a much   b many   c more

5 I'd _____ some of that, please.
   a want   b like   c have

6 Here you are. _____ else?
   a Nothing   b Something   c Anything

7 _____ six pounds eighty, please.
   a That's   b It's   c Here's

8 Here _____ go.
   a I   b you   c they

9 And _____ your change.
   a it's   b here's   c where's

4 ▶ 4.5 Listen to the three conversations again. Write 1, 2 or 3.

a The customer and the shop assistant are polite. _____

b The customer is <u>not</u> polite. _____

c The shop assistant is <u>not</u> polite. _____

HOME   BLOG   PODCASTS   ABOUT   CONTACT

Learning Curve

Tom and Sam talk about Marta's daily routine.

LISTENING

1 ▶ 4.6 Listen to the podcast about a person's daily routine. Tick (✔) the verbs you hear.

a get up   _____
b have a shower _____
c get dressed   _____
d have breakfast _____
e do housework   _____
f leave home   _____
g start work   _____
h finish work   _____
i get home   _____
j do homework   _____

2 ▶ 4.6 Listen again and choose the correct answers.

1 Where is Marta from?
   a France
   b Brazil
   c Spain

2 What time does Marta's day start?
   a 5.00
   b 5.15
   c 5.30

3 How does Marta travel to her daughter's house?
   a on the subway
   b by bike
   c by car

4 How far is Marta's house from her daughter's house?
   a five miles
   b ten miles
   c fifteen miles

5 What time does Marta's daughter arrive home?
   a 6.00
   b 6.30
   c 8.30

6 What does Marta do before she goes to bed?
   a She cooks a meal.
   b She watches TV.
   c She reads a book.

READING

1 Read Penny's blog about a long journey. How many types of transport does José tell her about?

a eight
b nine
c ten

2 Read the blog again. Write Y (Yes) or N (No).

1 Penny's family don't like her travel plans.   _____
2 José is Chilean.   _____
3 The bus from Lima to Cusco is expensive.   _____
4 The journey to Machu Picchu by car
   is easy.   _____
5 Most people go to La Paz by bike.   _____
6 José thinks the people in La Paz are nice.   _____
7 Walking tours in Santiago are cheap.   _____
8 Buenos Aires is a good city to see on foot.   _____

3 Match the adjectives with their opposites.

1 cold   _____   a unfriendly
2 noisy   _____   b quiet
3 fast   _____   c horrible
4 friendly _____   d cold
5 long   _____   e hot
6 nice   _____   f dirty
7 clean   _____   g slow
8 hot   _____   h short

HOME   BLOG   PODCASTS   ABOUT   CONTACT

Guest blogger Penny tells us about her latest travel plans.

A long journey

'It's a very bad idea.' That's what everyone says when I tell them my travel plans. And this is what my friends and family say when I tell them my new idea – to spend one month travelling from Lima in Peru to Buenos Aires in Argentina. 'It's dangerous!' says my mother. 'It's expensive!' says my father. 'It's really hot!' says one friend. 'It's really cold!' says another friend. Maybe they're right, but there is one thing I know – it's going to be an exciting trip!

It's a long journey and I don't want to be in a bus or car for a month. My plan is to use different types of transport on my trip. My friend José is from Mexico but he knows Peru and Chile very well. So, I asked him for help and he sent me this information. Thanks José!

OK Penny, you start your adventure in Lima. It's about seven hours from New York by plane. From Lima you go to the town of Cusco by bus. The bus is noisy and it's not fast but it's cheap. And there are beds! Cusco is famous because it's near Machu Picchu. The best way to get to Machu Picchu from Cusco is by train and then by foot. It is possible to go by car but don't – the roads are very bad! After Machu Picchu, take the train back to Cusco and your next stop is La Paz in Bolivia.

Most people travel to La Paz by bus but why don't you go by bike? You go around the beautiful Lake Titicaca. Stop for a day and see the lake by boat – it's an amazing place! Seven more days on your bike and you arrive in La Paz. Spend two or three days in La Paz because it's a very interesting city with friendly people.

I have an idea for the journey to Santiago in Chile – go by motorbike! It's a long journey (about four days) but the views are great. Santiago is another interesting city and the best way to see it is on foot. There are walking tours and they aren't expensive.

Your final journey is by train from Santiago to Buenos Aires. It's a long journey so go to the city of Mendoza by bus. Then take a different bus to Buenos Aires. The buses in Chile and Argentina are very nice and clean. Buenos Aires is a great city, but it is very big to see on foot. Travel on the subway to see everything.

What an exciting trip. Have fun!

All about me

GRAMMAR: can and can't

1 Complete the sentences and questions with can, can't and the verbs in the box.

> have   eat   read   start   study   ~~watch~~

1 A _____Can_____ we ____watch____ a film?
   B No, you ___can't___!

2 A I _____ _____ work at seven a.m. No problem.
   B That's great!

3 A _____ I _____ a shower?
   B Yes, you _____!

4 A He's only three but he _____ _____ books.
   B That's amazing!

5 A What's the problem?
   B It's very noisy! I _____ _____ in here!

6 A _____ your dog _____ chocolate?
   B No, he _____, it's bad for him.

2 Complete the conversations. Use can or can't and any other words you need.

1 'It's my brother's birthday tomorrow.' 'Really? I _____ a cake for him!'

2 'Can you speak Russian, Dominic?' 'Yes, _____. Why? Is that an email from your Russian friend?'

3 'Emma says she knows about computers but she _____ her new tablet.' 'I'm sure she _____. We _____ help her. It's easy!'

4 'We have some dollars, but we need euros in Paris. _____ some money at that bank?' 'No, _____. The bank isn't open today.'

5 'My grandfather is very old but he _____ a newspaper without glasses.' '_____ a car without them?'

6 'Can Sheila go shopping today? 'No, _____.

VOCABULARY: Common verbs (2)

3 Choose the correct verbs to complete the sentences.

I [1] call / speak / travel my grandmother every day, but on Wednesdays and Fridays I go to her house to [2] arrive / give / look after her because she can't [3] cook / give / help her own lunch. Sometimes my sister [4] speaks / helps / calls me, but usually I do it alone. My grandmother sometimes [5] dances / plays / sings the piano for me. She also likes to get out of the house, so I often [6] drive / arrive / travel her to the sea. She loves to [7] call / travel / swim in the sea. At weekends, she sometimes [8] helps / meets / sings her friends for a coffee.

4 Complete each pair of sentences with the same verb in the correct form.

1 A You must _____ at the airport two hours before your flight.
   B He always _____ late.

2 A She doesn't _____ the salsa but she's good at ballet.
   B I love this band! Do you want to _____ with me?

3 A My French isn't very good but I can _____ Polish.
   B Do you often _____ to your brothers?

4 A I _____ to different countries for my job.
   B It's easy to _____ to the city by train.

5 A Do the students _____ presents to their teachers?
   B He never _____ me back my pen after class!

6 A I can't _____ but I love listening to music.
   B It's a very difficult song to _____.

7 A The sea's too cold to _____ today.
   B I sometimes _____ in the pool in town.

PRONUNCIATION: can and can't

5 ▶ 5.1 Listen to the sentences. Write positive (+), negative (−) or question (?). Listen again, check and repeat.

1 ____   5 ____
2 ____   6 ____
3 ____   7 ____
4 ____   8 ____

LISTENING: Listening for specific information

1 Match sentences 1–6 with the pairs of photos a–f. Then complete the words with the missing vowels (a, e, i, o, u).

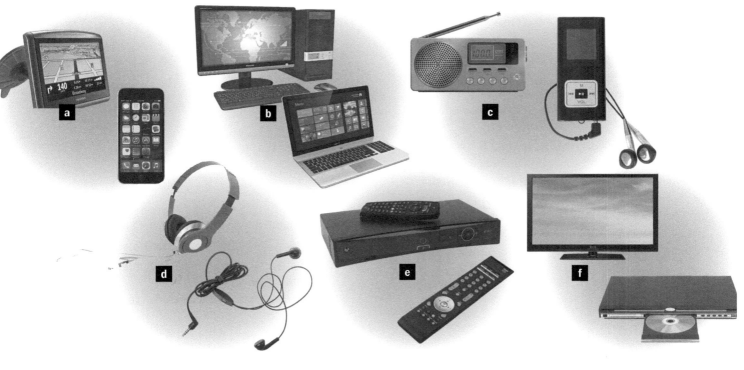

1 I don't have a d__skt__p c__mp__t__r,
   I have a l__pt__p.

2 Many people watch films on t__l__v__s__ __n from the internet but some also have DVD pl__y__rs.

3 I can't use __ __rph__n__s so I use h__ __dph__n__s to listen to music.

4 There's no need for a S__t N__v in your car if you own a sm__rtph__n__.

5 I listen to my MP3 pl__y__r or the r__d__ __ on the bus.

6 This r__m__t__ c__ntr__l is for the DVR – the 'd__g__t__l v__d__ __ r__c__rd__r'.

2 ▶5.2 Listen to a radio programme about technology. Choose the best title, a, b or c.

a Three reasons why people don't use technology.

b Three electronic devices people use.

c Three people with technology problems.

3 Read the sentences. Are the missing words a person, place, number or thing?

1 The speaker uses electronic technology for about ___number___ hours each day.

2 The speaker's _____ doesn't need a mobile device.

3 Many families can go on the internet in _____ different ways.

4 Some people think that the _____ is not safe.

5 They think that big internet companies want our personal _____.

6 People in the _____ look at screens for about nine hours every day.

4 ▶5.2 Listen again and complete the sentences in exercise 3.

5 ▶5.3 Read the sentences and underline the important words. Then listen, check and repeat.

1 My family comes from India but I live in Germany.

2 I can't buy the black laptop because it's too expensive.

3 That tablet is my sister's, not mine.

4 I study Spanish so I listen to Spanish radio online.

6 ▶5.4 Listen and write the important words.

1 I usually _____ _____ on my _____ before I _____ to _____.

2 Craig _____ _____ to _____ in his _____.

3 It says on the _____ that the _____ _____ at _____ o'clock.

GRAMMAR: Object pronouns

1 Choose the correct pronouns to complete the text.

Hi! My name's Gabriela but I don't like [1] *her / it / she*, so people call me Gabi. I'm 20 years old, and I'm a university student. There are lots of young people there, but I'm not like most of [2] *him / them / they*. They like dancing and enjoying themselves in the evening, but those things aren't fun for [3] *it / me / them*. I love sport, and I do [4] *it / they / us* with my friends, Piotr and Maggie. Piotr enjoys going out on his bike, so I often go cycling with [5] *he / her / him*. Maggie loves swimming, so I go with [6] *her / it / she* to the swimming pool every Tuesday. Why do we like exercise? Because it's good for [7] *it / us / we* and we're happy when we do [8] *it / them / him*. What about [9] *her / us / you*? Do you enjoy sport or do you hate [10] *him / it / me*?

2 Complete each sentence with one object pronoun and one subject pronoun.

1 Can I have your pen? I only need _____ for a minute. Oh, no, _____ 's red. I need a black one.

2 _____ don't speak Portuguese well but my friend Joao teaches _____ every week.

3 Evgeny and I like the same music. _____ normally listen to rap and R&B. Katerina likes the same music as _____ .

4 Excuse me, are _____ OK? Can I help _____ ?

5 I go to the gym with Juana. _____ takes me in her car. It's very good of _____ .

6 Lali and Naomi don't like the beach. It's too hot for _____ and _____ can't swim.

7 Michel studies English with me. _____ 's from Vietnam. I often see _____ after school.

8 Patricia is an actress. I sometimes see _____ on television but _____ isn't very famous.

VOCABULARY: Activities

3 ▶5.5 Listen and write the activities.

Jobs in the house	Sports
1 _____	3 _____
2 _____	4 _____

Evenings and weekends	Activities on your own
5 _____	7 _____
6 _____	_____
_____	8 _____

4 Complete each sentence with an activity.

1 She loves _____ but she doesn't have a bike!

2 _____ magazines is a great way to learn a new language.

3 There's no food in the house. We need to do some _____ today.

4 _____ in the sea is very cold in some countries!

5 I don't enjoy _____ at the cinema, but I like them on TV.

6 They're not good at _____ to disco music, but they like watching other people do it.

PRONUNCIATION: /h/

5 ▶5.6 Listen. Pay attention to the sound /h/. Listen again and repeat.

1 **A** How's your homework?
  B It's hard!

2 **A** She has lots of housework.
  B Can her husband help?

3 **A** Is Henry happy?
  B No, he hates his job.

4 **A** Hello. How is your holiday?
  B It's very hot!

5 **A** Are those his headphones?
  B No, they're Heidi's.

6 **A** When do you leave home?
  B At half past eight.

WRITING: Describing yourself

1 Read Margarita's profile. Which questions (1–7) does it answer? Write the paragraphs (A–D).

1 How do you travel around the city? _____
2 Where do you live? _____
3 What do you like doing in your free time? _____
4 What do you like watching on TV? _____
5 What job do you do? _____
6 What do you like to eat? _____
7 What jobs do your family do? _____

About me

a Hi! My name's Margarita, but you can call me Marga. I'm 26. I'm a police officer. It's an interesting job [1] _____.

b I live in Valparaiso, a city in Chile, near the capital, Santiago. Many tourists visit Valparaiso [2] _____. I live in the centre of the city in an apartment with my friend Jeremías.

c In my free time I like reading and cooking. I go running but I don't like it much [3] _____. But I love swimming. Valparaiso has a nice beach so I go there two or three times a week.

d My family are from Valparaiso. They live near me. I have two brothers and a little sister. My sister is at university. She studies IT [4] _____. My father and one of my brothers are police officers, like me. My other brother is a really good chef in an expensive restaurant, but I do the cooking when we are together at home [5] _____!

2 Match reasons a–g with gaps 1–5 in the profile. There are two extra reasons.

a because he thinks home cooking is too easy _____
b because I meet lots of different people and help them with their problems _____
c because the people are unfriendly _____
d because it's boring _____
e because she wants to be a computer programmer _____
f because I can't drive _____
g because it's a beautiful place near the sea _____

3 Write a personal profile for someone in your family, a friend, or a famous person. Make sure you:

- answer some of the questions in exercise 1.
- use paragraphs.
- give reasons with *because*.

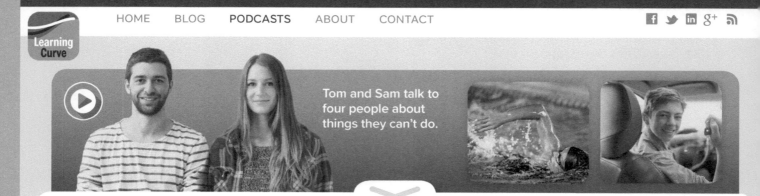

HOME   BLOG   **PODCASTS**   ABOUT   CONTACT

Learning Curve

Tom and Sam talk to four people about things they can't do.

LISTENING

1 ▶ **5.7** Listen to the podcast about things people can't do. Complete each sentence with one or two words.

1 Lorenzo can't _____.
2 Beatrice can't _____.
3 Ekaterina can't _____.
4 Robert can't _____.

2 ▶ **5.7** Listen again. Choose T (true) or F (false).

1 Sam thinks she can cook.   T / F
2 Lorenzo doesn't have a car.   T / F
3 Lorenzo's friends never go to the beach.   T / F
4 Beatrice can't dance.   T / F
5 Ekaterina's daughter can swim.   T / F
6 Ekaterina wants to learn how to swim.   T / F
7 Robert can speak Polish.   T / F
8 Robert wants a French teacher.   T / F

3 Write the common verbs.

1 Can you p_____ any musical instruments?
2 Let's m_____ this afternoon outside school.
3 I can dance well, but I can't s_____at all!
4 When you get home this evening, c_____ me.
5 Which countries do you want to t_____ to in the future?
6 I sometimes l_____ a_____ my grandparents' dog.
7 Please h_____ me to carry these bags into the house.
8 What time does the bus a_____ in the city centre?

READING

1 Read Marc's blog about technology. Match the sentences with gaps 1–3.

a The study also shows that young people use technology in a very different way to old people.
b It tells us that young people today have different technology to older people.
c Another difference is the amount of time we spend using technology.

2 Read the blog again. Choose the correct words to complete the sentences.

1 The survey asks people _____ questions.
  a three
  b four
  c five

2 _____ of older people own an MP3 player.
  a 26%
  b 60%
  c 74%

3 People of different ages all use _____.
  a headphones
  b computers
  c the internet

4 Marc's grandmother _____ every evening.
  a listens to the radio
  b watches TV
  c goes online

5 Old and young people use their smartphones to _____.
  a take photos
  b make calls
  c watch videos

6 Marc thinks older people play games because _____.
  a they have money
  b they don't work
  c the games are free

HOME   **BLOG**   PODCASTS   ABOUT   CONTACT

Our guest blogger Marc looks at the different ways young and old people use technology.

Technology for the **young** and **old**

How old are you? What technology do you have? What do you use it for? How often do you use it? A new survey in the USA asks people these questions and here are some of the results.

1 _____

Can you guess the answer to this question: Which group has more desktop computers: people aged 18–34 or people aged 57–65? The answer is interesting – it's the older group. Can you guess why? It's because young people have laptops and phones. They don't need desktop computers! Another interesting result of the survey is about music. Only 26% of people aged 60 and above have an MP3 player. For people in their twenties it's 74%. But does this mean old people don't listen to music? Of course not! My parents often listen to music but they do it at home. And they like the same music so they never need headphones!

2 _____

The survey says that almost all ages use the internet. I think that's interesting because some people think that the internet is only for young people. In fact, only very old people don't go online. But young people do spend more time online than older people. This doesn't surprise me – most of my friends spend hours on the internet every day. A lot of us need it for our jobs. But I think old people spend a lot of time using other technology. My grandmother is nearly 80. It's true that she never goes online – she doesn't even have a computer! But she loves listening to the radio and she watches TV for hours every evening. She's very fast with the remote control!

3 _____

One fact from the survey is that most older people only use their smartphones for one or two things. But young people make calls, send messages, go online, buy things, listen to music and watch videos – all on their smartphones. Both age groups use their smartphones to take photos, but the type of photos is different. Young people love to take selfies! Another fact from the survey was about social media. Old people use it to find old friends and chat with their families. Young people use social media to find new friends. But my favourite fact from the survey was this: it says that old people play a lot of free games online! I think I know why this is – they don't have jobs. It's easy to play games when you have a lot of time!

WRITING: Completing a form

1 ▶ WP1   Listen to the conversation at a bus station. Complete the 'lost property' form.

Greyford Bus Services	Personal details
Title: Mr [✓] Mrs [ ] Ms [ ]	
First name: *Anthony*	Surname: ¹_____
Address: ²_____ *Fairmead Road*	Email address: ⁴_____@starmail.com
Town/City: ³_____	Phone number: *07593 8103327*
Post code: *PD2 9BV*	Date of birth (DD/MM/YYYY): *15/03/* ⁵_____
Details of lost item	
Object: *brown wallet with £40 and credit card*	
Date lost: *13/02/2018 at about 9.30 a.m*	
Place lost: *bus number* ⁶_____	

2 ▶ WP2   Listen to another conversation and correct five pieces of information.

Greyford Bus Services	Personal details
Title: Mr [ ] Mrs [✓] Ms [ ]	
First name: *Nithya*	Surname: *Patil*
Address: *55 Old Street*	Email address: *nithya@padmail.co.uk*
Town/City: *Greyford*	Phone number: *05387 7729055*
Post code: *GY7 2HU*	Date of birth (DD/MM/YYYY): *01/02/1989*

3 Write the sentences again with capital letters where you need them.

1 he's in the u.s.a but he's japanese.

_____

2 i am from rouen, in france.

_____

3 my post code is n2 r45.

_____

4 his sister speaks polish and french.

_____

5 these are michael's keys.

_____

6 she lives at number 6, green street.

_____

4 Complete Michi's form with the information in the box. Use capital letters where you need them.

> 01656 388 9846   mrs fujioka   31/08/2000   cromton   40, park road
> cr8 9ev   japanese   m_fujioka@starmail.jp   michi

Personal details			
Title	¹_____	Post code	⁶_____
First name	²_____	Email address	⁷_____
Surname	³_____	Phone number	⁸_____
Address	⁴_____	Nationality	⁹_____
Town/City	⁵_____	Date of birth (DD/MM/YYYY) ¹⁰_____	

WRITING: Punctuation

1 Read the blog post about three men's journeys to work or school. Match the names with the reasons they travel so far (a–c).

1 Joshua ____   a His family lives far from where he works/studies.

2 David ____   b He doesn't have the money to live near where he works/studies.

3 Pat ____   c He doesn't want to live near where he works/studies.

Stories of the daily commute*

I'm Joshua. ¹_____ In fact, it takes me over an hour and fifteen minutes to get to work. ²_____ I do it because the good jobs are in the city but it's expensive to live there. But why do other people commute long distances?

David Givens has one of the longest commutes in the United States – 600 kilometres a day from the mountains in Mariposa County to San Jose. It's a journey of three and a half hours each way, but David says it's great because his life in Mariposa is so wonderful and he prefers it to San Jose. ³_____

Pat Skinner leaves home at seven to drive 80 kilometres. ⁴_____ But Pat isn't an office worker commuting to work, he's an eleven-year-old schoolboy. His mum drives him about 500 km each week so that he can go to a good private school. He does his homework in the car!

How far do you commute each day? ⁵_____ Comment below!

*commute – (n and v) journey to work every day

2 Add the punctuation to these sentences. Then match them with gaps 1–5 in the blog in exercise 1.

a at seven in the evening he gets home

b davids house is in the mountains its a clean place far from the cities of the coast

c do you like your journey to work

d every morning i cycle to the station and get on a busy train into the city

e I work in london and like many people i spend a lot of my day between home and work

3 Complete the sentences with *and* or *but*.

1 He usually cycles _____ today he's on the bus.

2 Why does Andy walk to work _____ take the train home?

3 Every morning, Breana buys a coffee _____ a cake at the station.

4 I live _____ work in the same town, so I don't travel far every day.

5 My mother's office is in the city, _____ on Fridays she works at home.

6 They work in the same office _____ go to work together.

4 You are going to write a blog post about a journey you often make (every day/week/month). Use these questions to plan your writing.

• Where do you go?

• How far is the journey (minutes and hours or kilometres)?

• How do you travel?

• Do you enjoy it? Why/Why not?

• Do you travel with other people?

• What do you see on the journey?

• Is the journey expensive/interesting/difficult, etc?

5 Write your blog post.

• use correct punctuation and capital letters correctly.

• use the linkers *and* and *but*.

WRITING: Describing yourself

1 Read Olga's personal profile. Then match questions a–f with paragraphs 1–4. There are two extra questions.

a What are you good at? ____

b What are your hobbies? ____

c What's your family like? ____

d What's your plan in the next five years? ____

e Where do you live and what's it like? ____

f Who are you and what do you do? ____

LET'S LEARN A LANGUAGE!

Olga St Petersburg

1 Hi everyone. I'm Olga from Russia. I'm nineteen. At the moment I'm a student at university. I'm studying teaching and I plan to teach languages one day.

2 I'm from Yekaterinburg but I study in St Petersburg, Russia's second city. I don't have my own apartment – this city is very expensive – but I share a big flat with four other students. It's near to the university, the park and a large shopping centre. St Petersburg is a beautiful city for nine months of the year but it can get very cold and dark around January!

3 In my spare time, I enjoy reading, listening to music and learning languages – I speak three already and my Portuguese is OK. Why do I want to improve my English? Because it lets me speak to the world and because I need it if I want to work in a good school.

4 I don't see my family very often because I live so far from home. I have an older brother – he works as a doctor in Yekaterinburg and he has two lovely children. My younger brother is at school and lives with my parents. My dad is an engineer and my mum works at home.

2 Read the profile again. Write T (true) or F (false).

1 Olga has a job in a school. ____

2 She doesn't live in her home city. ____

3 Five people live in her flat. ____

4 St Petersburg is a lovely place to live all year. ____

5 She only learns languages because she wants to. ____

6 She has two brothers. ____

7 Her father is a doctor. ____

8 The website is for people who want to learn languages. ____

3 Use the prompts to write sentences with *because*.

1 Abbey / never / go / dancing / very expensive

_____.

2 I / not need / a car / there / shop / near / our house

_____.

3 Jamie / love / weekends / he / sleep / late

_____!

4 Why / she / do / yoga / ? / want / make friends

_____

5 I / can / run / today / have / bad knee

_____

6 Why / I / like / this cinema / ? / cheap

_____!

4 Write a personal profile for a language exchange website.

• use paragraphs

• say the language(s) you speak and the language you want to practise

• give reasons with *because*.

Richmond

58 St Aldates
Oxford
OX1 1ST
United Kingdom

Second reprint: 2024
ISBN: 978-84-668-2601-3
CP: 881093

© Richmond / Santillana Global S.L. 2018

Publishing Director: Deborah Tricker

Publisher: Simone Foster

Media Publisher: Sue Ashcroft

Workbook Publisher: Luke Baxter

Content Developer: David Cole-Powney

Editors: Sue Jones, Debra Emmett, Tom Hadland, Fiona Hunt, Laura Miranda, Helen Wendholt

Proofreaders: Pippa Mayfield, Shannon Niell, Jamie Bowman, Amanda Leigh

Design Manager: Lorna Heaslip

Cover Design: This Ain't Rock'n'Roll, London

Design & Layout: Lorna Heaslip, Dave Kuzmicki, emc design Ltd.

Photo Researcher: Magdalena Mayo

Learning Curve video: Mannic Media

Audio production: Tom, Dick and Debbie, TEFL Audio

App development: The Distance

We would also like to thank the following people for their valuable contribution to writing and developing the material:
Pamela Vittorio (Video Script Writer), Belen Fernandez (App Project Manager), Eleanor Clements (App Content Creator)

We would like to thank all those who have given their kind permission to reproduce material for this book:

Illustrators:

Simon Clare; Guillaume Gennet; Paul Dickinson c/o Lemonade; John Goodwin; Sean Longcroft c/o KJA Artists; The Boy Fitzhammond c/o NB Illustration Ltd.

Photos:

J. Escandell.com; J. Jaime; J. Lucas; S. Enríquez; 123RF; ALAMY/GerryRousseau, Jim Corwin, Moviestore collection Ltd, Simon Reddy, Stephen French, IanDagnall Computing, Joern Sackermann, dpa picture alliance, Serhii Kucher, ZUMA Press, Inc., All Canada Photos, London Entertainment, Everett Collection Inc, imageBROKER, Pongpun Ampawa, Peter Noyce GBR, Ian Allenden, AF archive, Elizabeth Livermore, Lex Rayton, Ted Foxx, Alvey & Towers Picture Library, Elizabeth Wake, Kristoffer Tripplaar, Lucas Vallecillos, Joe Fairs, Dinodia Photos, Peter D Noyce, Brigette Supernova, Pictorial Press Ltd, Collection Christophel, Jonathan Goldberg, Paul Hastie, Tierfotoagentur, REUTERS, Viktor Fischer, Art of Food, Andrey Armyagov, Alex Ramsay, Blend Images, B Christopher, Judith Collins, David Cabrera Navarro, Roman Tiraspolsky, robertharding, Michael Neelon(misc), Fredrick Kippe, Oleksiy Maksymenko Photography, Patti McConville, D. Callcut, Matthew Taylor, Rafael Angel Irusta Machin, Igor Kovalchuk, MallorcaImages, Paul Quayle, Jozef Polc, Mick Sinclair, Michael Willis, Hugh Threlfall, ITAR-TASS Photo Agency, Bailey-Cooper Photography, jeremy sutton-hibbert, creativep, James Jeffrey Taylor, Oleksiy Maksymenko, Paul Smith, David Levenson, United Archives GmbH, Justin Kase zsixz, Simon Dack, Jeremy Pembrey, Barry Diomede, Alex Linch, Tomas Abad, Valentin Luggen, Sergey Soldatov, Iakov Filimonov, Anton Gvozdikov, Alex Segre, MBI, Paul Gibson, Stocksolutions, MEDIUM FORMAT COLLECTION/Balan Madhavan, allesalltag, David Robertson, Dmytro Zinkevych, Simon Dack News, Vaidas Bucys; CATERS NEWS AGENCY; FOCOLTONE; GETTY IMAGES SALES SPAIN/bjdlzx, Yuri_Arcurs, Reenya, Nikada, Paul Almasy, Martin Rose, Maskot, Lars Baron, JamieB, Annie Engel, Fosin2, Darumo, BraunS, artisticco, ajr_images, Bison_, AzmanL, artursfoto, pringletta, Dobino, Berezka_Klo, Indeed, Hero Images, KingWu, Tom Merton, NI QIN, Sam Edwards, Portra, ajaykampani, bgblue, leungchopan, c_kawi, s-c-s, kali9, SensorSpot,

LeoPatrizi, Talaj, Pix11, Neyya, Dan Dalton, Chimpinski, DKart, shank_ali, Chris Ryan, londoneye, kickstand, kiankhoon, joto, Fuse, skynesher, asbe, gavran333, Zinkevych, KJA, AFP, ViewStock, John Lund/Sam Diephuis, Hiya Images/Corbis/VCG, Tom Dulat, vm, imaginima, TF-Images, Ben Pipe Photography, Ridofranz, PPcavalry, Edda Dupree / EyeEm, Dave Hogan/MTV 2016, Lightcome, Isovector, VikramRaghuvanshi, FaraFaran, Cimmerian, Bet_Noire, David C Tomlinson, Dave & Les Jacobs, unaemlag, technotr, Zoran Kolundzija, tarras79, stockcam, MacLife Magazine, Jetta Productions, Maya Karkalicheva, DGLimages, innovatedcaptures, FatCamera, Power Sport Images, Jasmina81, Lorraine Boogich, Mirrorpix, Kevin C. Cox - FIFA, Purestock, Caiaimage/ Tom Merton, Stockbyte, Jason England / EyeEm, Ted Soqui, scyther5, Steven Swinnen / EyeEm, Weedezign, Westend61, Dave and Les Jacobs/Kolostock, chachamal, Cultura RM Exclusive/Frank and Helena, Echo, imagotres, julief514, karandaev, kpalimski, demaerre, Danny Martindale, Art-Y, omda_info, colematt, clubfoto, Allan Tannenbaum, DNY59, stevecoleimages, David Lees, DonNichols, JB Lacroix, asiseeit, Tuutikka, Tarzhanova, Thinkstock, Vladimir Godnik, Uwe Krejci, Venturelli, VladTeodor, Synergee, NurPhoto, Samuel de Roman, nycshooter, RuslanDashinsky, sorincolac, AndreyPopov, AngiePhotos, MistikaS, JGalione, Choreograph, Fotoplanner, Leah Puttkammer, Hero images, John Keeble, Liam Norris, JANIFEST, LWA/Dann Tardif, Ron Galella, Rose_Carson, IvanMiladinovic, Shana Novak, Simon Sarin, T3 Magazine, Floortje, Hung_Chung_Chih, artlensfoto, domin_domin, Frank van Delft, macrovector, michaeljung, penguenstok, Flashpop, DenisKot, Wavebreakmedia, Creative, Claudiad, Sheikoevgeniya, Philipp Nemenz, Bettmann, Al Freni, EmirMemedovski, wir0man, pshonka, Anthony Harvey, Anadolu Agency, mrak_hr, mixetto, i love images, mbbirdy, kivoart, SnegiriBureau, Rick Friedman, jsnover, iconeer, Monty Rakusen, gilaxia, Maksim Ozerov, gerenme, MStudioImages, MATJAZ SLANIC, andresr, Jupiterimages, Jon Feingersh, adekvat, Jamie Garbutt, Jack Mitchell, Mark Cuthbert, R-O-M-A, Paras Griffin, Peathegee Inc, Radius Images, Gabriel Rossi, FrozenShutter, blueringmedia, davidcreacion, NuStock, justhavealook, reportman1985, zeljkosantrac, Dougal Waters, David Redfern, Askold Romanov, Digital Vision, Krasyuk, Javier Pierini, Marc Romanelli, Neustockimages, Andersen Ross, Alistair Berg, Steven Puetzer, Todor Tsvetkov, Devonyu, franckreporter, Anthony Charles, Danita Delimont, senkoumelnik, ferrantraite, Chesnot, ersinksacik, bluejayphoto, NicolasMcComber, Photos.com Plus, Robyn Mackenzie, Astarot, Tony Vaccaro, Santiago Felipe, Tristan Fewings, Tetra Images, dogayusufdokdok, nicoletaionescu, praetorianphoto, vgajic, Sofie Delauw, Birgit R / EyeEm, Christopher Polk, PeopleImages, Henn Photography, KavalenkavaVolha, Kittisak_Taramas, sturti, Mike Coppola, Nicolas McComber, Tatjana Kaufmann, LuisPortugal, christopherarndt, Adrian Weinbrecht, Chris Sattlberger, subjug, JuliarStudio, Juice Images, Jrg Mikus / EyeEm, sturti, Roberto Westbrook, Tanya Constantine, Valery Sharifulin, Jason Hawkes, Image Source, IMAGEMORE Co, Ltd., Jacob Wackerhausen, seb_ra, crossroadscreative, m-imagephotography, DEA PICTURE LIBRARY, Hiroyuki Ito, Erik Isakson, EvgeniyaTiplyashina, Hill Street Studios, lushik, Mondadori Portfolio, Andreas Hein / EyeEm, Axelle/Bauer-Griffin, Emad Aljumah, Deborah Kolb, monkeybusinessimages, Alexandr Sherstobitov, laflor, Michael Ochs Archives, Science Photo Library, BJI / Blue Jean Images, Dan MacMedan, ChrisHepburn, kzenon, Banar Fil Ardhi / EyeEm, PhotoAlto/Sigrid Olsson, Jade Albert Studio, Inc., New York Daily News Archive, Constantinos Kollias / EyeEm, Chris Walter, Photo by Claude-Olivier Marti, Kelly Cheng Travel Photography, Blend Images - Jose Luis Pelaez Inc, shapecharge, Compassionate Eye Foundation/Steven Errico, gbh007; HIGHRES PRESS STOCK/AbleStock.com; I. PREYSLER; ISTOCKPHOTO/ Getty Images Sales Spain, Devasahayam Chandra Dhas, Andreas Herpens, calvindexter, popovaphoto, Phazemedia, denphumi, SolStock, Pali Rao, JoeLena; J. M.ª BARRES; SHUTTERSTOCK/ Glenn Copus/Evening Standard, Olivia Rutherford, MARIUS ALEXANDER, Iakov Filimonov, Sergey Novikov, Blend Images, terekhov igor; Farmer's Daughter; Jono Williams; Andrew Hyde; Aimee Giese; Museum of London; Samsung; SERIDEC PHOTOIMAGENES CD; Telegraph Media Group Limited; Prats i Camps; 123RF; ALAMY/David South, Peter M. Wilson, SuperStock, Felix Lipov, VIEW Pictures Ltd, Hugh Threlfall, Zaid Saadallah, Cultura Creative (RF), Jon Davison, Af8images, Vincent de Vries photography, David Willis, Jenny Matthews, age fotostock, Igor Kovalchuk, ONOKY - Photononstop; GETTY IMAGES SALES SPAIN/cnythzl, David Leahy, NuStock, Thinkstock, kanate, Time & Life Pictures, Grafissimo, zetter, Hero Images, Yapanda, ozgurdonmaz, greg801, Michael Heim / EyeEm, artapornp, Indeed, Csondy, JTB Photo, AzmanL, aomam, FaberrInk, LauriPatterson, Jordan Siemens, Hermsdorf, Innocenti, Icon Sports Wire, Lily Chou, Mike Kemp, Zou Yanju, Baloncici, plherrera, unalozmen, Daebarpapa, Fuse, pixdeluxe, pixelliebe, AndreyPopov, quavondo, mactrunk, Komkrit2101, Yuri_Arcurs, clu, vectorikart, Getty Images, John Freeman, SolStock, ROSLAN RAHMAN, Paul Bradbury, Pingebat, Monty Rakusen, Jupiterimages, Niteenrk, Jodi Jacobson, Gabriel Rossi, Dan Bass, Sascha Kilmer, Siri Stafford, i love images, jarenwicklund, Hulton Deutsch, Jeff Greenberg, Toby Burrows, Tetra Images, Letizia Le Fur, Neustockimages, Richard Levine, StockPhotosArt, Alasdair Turner, Photos.com, Plus, Comstock, Veronica Garbutt, Agencia Makro/CON, Claudio Ventrella, LightFieldStudios, DEA PICTURE LIBRARY, Hill Street Studios, Jose Luis Pelaez Inc, Min Geolshik, Johnny Greig, Matteo Lepore / EyeEm, Top Photo Corporation, RubberBall Productions, Wild Horse Photography, Blend Images - Terry Vine, Scott Polar Research Institute, University of Cambridge, smirart; ISTOCKPHOTO Getty Images Sales Spain, shapecharge, kyoshino; TOMTOM; ARCHIVO SANTILLANA

Cover Photo: GETTY IMAGES SALES SPAIN/mixetto

We would like to thank the following reviewers for their valuable feedback which has made Personal Best possible. We extend our thanks to the many teachers and students not mentioned here.
Brad Bawtinheimer, Manuel Hidalgo, Paulo Dantas, Diana Bermúdez, Laura Gutiérrez, Hardy Griffin, Angi Conti, Christopher Morabito, Hande Kokce, Jorge Lobato, Leonardo Mercato, Mercilinda Ortiz, Wendy López

Printed in Brazil by Forma Certa Gráfica Digital
Lote: 800.421